CHAOS TO REINVENTION

CHAOS TO REINVENTION

How to Turn Chaos into Clarity

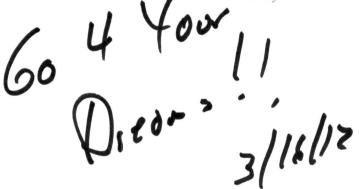

Go 4 Your Dreams!!

3/16/12

Jerry Isenhour

ISBN-13: 9781539500117
ISBN-10: 153950011X
Library of Congress Control Number: 2016917220
CreateSpace Independent Publishing Platform
North Charleston, South Carolina

Table of Contents

Dedication

There are people in your life who are there to pick you up when you fall, to believe in you when you lack belief in yourself, and who are the people who truly help you through the stumbles we suffer in life. I have dedicated this book to some who played not only a part of my reinvention but also were the people who made me believe in myself.

My Wife Sheryl, who was there to support every day since the day we met, with her as my best friend and soulmate, she was there to tell me that brighter days would come.

My friend and mentor John Meredith, the man who steered me when I had no idea what was next in life and who gave me the courage and strength.

To Ken Warren, a guy who was there with me as a brother at many points in my life.

To Roger Charron, he left this world too young, but was a brother of another Mother to me while here on God's green earth

To Greg Polakow, he was there as a friend and was the writer who helped me with this project and who has served as a ghostwriter for me for many years

To my children and grandchildren, each with their own dreams and hopes

To my clients, those who believed in me and have allowed me the greatest privilege anyone could every share, that of helping them on the journey to their dreams

And to the chimney sweep industry of America and abroad, a great group of people who are an extended family to me where no matter where I travel a colleague and friend can always be found

Chaos—complete disorder and utter confusion.

Reinvention—to transform into the right model that fills the need.

So often failure will halt people, and from that point forward the fear of failure will stifle their imagination and be a set of brakes on their drive.

> *If you're not failing every now and then, it's a sign you're not doing anything very innovative.*
>
> —WOODY ALLEN

Introduction

This book details three very important episodes in my business and personal life. These separate but related episodes, while deeply challenging at times, provided the impetus for the quality of my personal life today and my successful and gratifying transition to a new career, a redefined sense of purpose, and a reinvigorated understanding of my life's mission. The value they may hold for a reader are the lessons I learned about life, business, perseverance, coping, and appreciation for those around me as I navigated my way through.

The first of these episodes describes how I built three related, highly successful, profitable businesses: a chimney service business, a hearth retail business, and a manufacturing business for outdoor products—this was done with the support of spouses and others. The second episode details how totally and swiftly these businesses and our lives were subjected to immense upheaval by the widespread financial chaos that began in September of 2008. The third episode details how, together, we overcame the very destructive, shattering experience of this upheaval and moved into a new and immensely fulfilling phase of our lives and careers.

> *Try not to be a man of success, but rather become a man of value.*

—ALBERT EINSTEIN

September 28, 2008, The Day
The World Changed

I still remember clearly what I was doing on this day. I was scouting a new location for a hearth and outdoor living retail showroom. My plans at the time were to include a new state-of-the-art showroom for outdoor living that would become a model for the industry. The location appeared to be right, the timing was on track, the economy was booming (or so it seemed), business was great, and demand for outdoor living products was at an all-time high. It was, in short, a perfect time for us and this new endeavor. Or so we thought. We didn't realize then that miles away, in our nation's capital of Washington, DC, the financial world was about to take a big hit—some may compare it to a nuclear hit. It was a hit that would disrupt our lives, our businesses, and the entire global economy in ways that, at the time, we could not even imagine. Even now, looking back on all the consequences of this event, it seems hard to believe these things could happen. This day was the beginning of the end of the American dream for many, and we were going to suffer through the upcoming events in a most adverse way.

I remember how optimistic I felt as Sheryl and I surveyed this great piece of property in a rapidly growing section of town. The talk of the entire area was how a new access road to the interstate was going to be a gateway to the new developments in the nearby town of Kannapolis, North Carolina. Multibillionaire David Murdock was in the process of building the North Carolina Research Campus there, and a brand-new four-lane highway was expected to move people to this center of research. Large, high-end neighborhoods full of million-dollar homes were constructed, some built on a custom basis, others built for the speculative market of what was assured to be coming.

Filled with visions and expectations about this new venture and this perfect site, we went to a nearby restaurant for lunch. I even remember ordering a cheeseburger, fries, and an iced tea. (It's funny how those little details stick in your mind even as your world is about to be destroyed.) The television was on CNN and it was displaying the congressional vote for the first bank bailout bill. When the roll call was announced, the bill was defeated. The first bank bailout bid had failed in the House of Representatives.

Now we had heard things about banks having issues and that some of them had been designated as stressed by the Federal Reserve System and the Federal Deposit Insurance Corporation, but this had not seemed to slow the economy. I mean, who pays attention to the news stories? Bad things today are quickly forgotten within days.

It seemed almost inconsequential to us at the time, but the effects of this congressional vote resulted in the first-ever trillion-dollar-plus stock market loss. Stocks bottomed out, and the price of gold went to over $900 an ounce very quickly. The effects of this day were devastating to the global economy. New construction halted and most damaging of all, money and credit dried up. And this seemed to happen overnight, even though it had been coming on and none of us had paid attention. I mean, after all, the economy was performing at a record level; our biggest challenge had been simply to find workers.

At the time we had no clear idea what these events would mean in our lives, but I quickly lost my appetite for some reason. I remember looking at Sheryl and telling her, "I think we are screwed. This is going to change *everything*." How little did I realize then just how accurate that prediction would be. Little did I know that from that day forward, the entire world, most especially my own, was headed to the dump, and it was on a high-speed locomotive to drive it there.

This was the day that chaos started—a chaos that would not end for many years. I simply had no way to conceive of the overwhelming, gut-wrenching difficulties these events would bring to us. I also had no notion at all that my own past actions in business were going to play a huge role in my downfall.

You see, I had become an expert at how to run a business with bank money. Why? Because credit was easy, and there was always more whenever we needed it. But the unintended consequence of that environment was that our position was far from liquid. In fact, we were somewhere at the opposite end of the spectrum. Our businesses and our personal lives were structured on what, at the time, seemed like an indestructible supply of credit. That situation was about to change, and it would have a devastating effect on our lives.

> *My fault, my failure, is not in the passions I have,*
> *but rather in my lack of control of them.*

—JACK KEROUAC

Childhood; The Period That Forms Life's Direction

Tell people there is an invisible man in the sky who invented the universe, and the vast majority will believe you. Tell them the paint is wet, and they have to touch it to be sure.

—George Carlin

Many years prior to that eventful day, I had decided to become self-employed. Throughout my childhood and teenage years, I had always been on a mission to establish my own business, make my own way in the world, and be independent.

I didn't deal well with supervision. So during my years of growing up, I established a lot of small enterprises. One was washing cars at a nearby service station. I cut a deal with the owner to pay him fifty cents for each car I washed. At the age of twelve, I was washing eight to twelve cars every Saturday for three dollars each. I was also doing detailing for about ten dollars. That was a lot of money at the time. The minimum wage was a little over a dollar an hour. So by comparison, my small car-washing enterprise was one that paid a hefty return.

The amazing thing about this was that I was the first person in my family who had ever been self-employed. My other family members held traditional jobs. My mother worked in an auto parts store and later in a bank, my father worked as a police officer the majority of his life, my stepfather was a truck driver, and my stepmother was a secretary in the school system. Even more extended family all held jobs. None, for some reason, had ever entered the world of self-employment; having done so myself, I was an oddity among my family members.

Traditional school subjects held no interest for me, so when I entered high school, I enrolled in a vocational training class—Industrial Cooperative Training also known as ICT. Its purpose was to prepare people for the workforce in industrial settings, or blue-collar work. In this ICT program, you went to school for only half a day and had a job for the rest of the day. You were graded on your job performance. And getting out of school at lunchtime was certainly an appeal to me.

My instructor, J. Lee Hopkins, shared with me that he had a local printing company interested in the program and wanted to bring in a few students to train in the printing industry. Well, this sounded a whole lot more appealing than the cotton mill.

In the small southern mill town where I lived, this kind of preparation of working in industrial settings was common as a part of a high school education. The mill tended to dominate the economy of towns like this and was almost always the principal employer. In those days, the mills were king in the South. As a result, many of my classmates were employed by the cotton or hosiery mills of the area. My grandmother had worked in a cotton mill from the time she was twelve until the day she retired at sixty-five. She had worked on looms by standing on a crate as a child in the early part of the twentieth century. Child labor was common in those days. I think even as a child I had no desire to be an employee of one of the local textile mills. Maybe it was my memory of the mill's window screens being clogged with cotton lint, or maybe it was the fact that the people who worked in the mills were called lintheads because when they left the mills in the evening, their hair was coated with cotton lint.

In fact, these people seemed to me like robots. They walked into the mill every day at the same exact time when the whistle blew and then walked back out when it blew again later in the afternoon. Each one carried a lunch box. Each wore the same clothes every day. It may have been a job for them, but watching them shuffle by the gate guard both coming and going, day in and day out, reminded me more of a prison. It was not a work group I had any desire to join.

My grandmother lived in a tiny mill house a block from the mill, and she worked the third shift her entire life while she raised my mother, my aunt, and three of my uncles. Her house had no hot water, no central heat, or any of the other things that today we would consider as fundamental for basic comfort. Nevertheless, my grandmother was very happy, and as a small child I was often looked after by her. I think I was her favorite grandchild since the others lived in other towns and she seldom saw them. I walked to her house every day after grammar school. But one thing was apparent to me: Going to work in a cotton or hosiery mill would likely doom me to what I saw around me every day. Some years later, when the movie *Norma Rae* came out with Sally Field in the lead role, the thoughts of growing up and living in millhouses came back to my mind and once again reminded me that this job did not match my vision in life.

The local economy, centered around mills, was doomed and destined to change; textiles today are mostly an imported product, with a dwindling percentage manufactured in this country. How well I remember when the mills started to close and thousands of people had no other training and nowhere to go. It proved correct; it was a good decision to choose another trade as I was going through my high school years.

The printing job appealed to me. At least it was something different. I knew I wanted no part of what appeared to be the robotic life of a linthead.

The best way to predict your future is to create it.

—Abraham Lincoln

3

The First Real Job

The local printing company was called Snyder Printing. It had been around for many years. I learned a trade from these fine people, who truly cared for their employees. I still remember the first night I worked there. It had about thirty employees, but David Snyder taught me how to run a Kluge printing press that had been adapted to run the gold foil stamping process. It still amazes me that David, the owner's son, was down in the lower levels of his family's printing business patiently sharing with a sixteen-year-old kid how to run this printing press.

As I completed my final two years of high school, it was evident that I was well suited to printing. But I wanted more, much more. So, while still in high school, I went to work for two other printing companies, driving to Charlotte every day (about a forty-five-minute commute each way) and working the second shift at printing companies as a helper on a multicolor offset press. But I had bigger goals. I wanted to be a pressman. A pressman was the king of the print shop.

When I graduated from high school, I left the printing company for which I had been working and got a job at a different one on the second shift running a two-color, thirty-eight-inch printing press. I was hired as a pressman, and my dream was realized. This may not sound like much to most people, but it was quite an accomplishment for an eighteen-year-old kid fresh out of high school. Most of the guys running these were much older, I was just a kid, many had children older than me. But I was a smart-ass, cocky guy who was on a path to prove to the world I could do it. The world was anyone who would watch me.

During this time frame I got married, children were born, and we relocated to an apartment on the south side of Charlotte.

While living there, a nightmare occurred. At the completion of my shift one night, without any idea this was going to happen, my supervisor called me aside to tell me I was being fired. This hit me like a ton of bricks. But from his discussion with me, I found out that something about my attitude made managers feel that I did not fit the company's expected model. Here I was in a strange town, with a wife who was a stay-at-home mom, two small kids, no savings, and suddenly no job. The situation might have been my introduction to chaos, but as it turned out, it wasn't. Since I had acquired a highly valued skill as an offset pressman, by midday the following day I had a new job. Chaos had been easily averted. In fact, I was even going to make more money. Why did I get fired? Well, I was a really hard person to supervise and wasn't a good follower. Perhaps you will be able to grasp this for yourself later in my story as my fall into chaos becomes clear.

Perhaps if I had suffered more pain at that time, I might have become more keenly aware of the ever-present possibility of being brought low by life's unforeseen circumstances. If that had happened, I might have been able to avoid some of the circumstances that were to lead to much greater upheaval and a lot more pain. But I got off easy—that time. So if anything, I felt a bit cockier about myself than before. At the time of my firing, I had a safety blanket—my mother. Throughout my life, each and every time I was ever in need, my mother was there. My mother, who believed I could do no wrong, often bailed me out of financial trouble.

A great example of this was the time I decided to buy a boat. As a young man of twenty-one, several things did not register in my brain as I made this purchase. One was the minor detail that I could not afford the eighty-nine-dollar monthly boat payment. Even worse, somehow I had overlooked the reality that my Chevrolet Vega GT, with its four-cylinder engine, was not exactly ideal for pulling a ski boat anywhere, much less up a boat ramp. My mother bailed her foolish son out by paying for the boat. This, then, was another escape from my impulsiveness with little or no harm done.

I have come to realize it is not always wise to intercede on behalf of your children when they make mistakes. Sometimes it is better to let them experience the consequences of bad decisions. It's one of the ways they learn, one of the ways they grow up. Although I deeply valued my mother's constant willingness to save my bacon, I wonder if, in the long run, it might have been better if she had allowed me to flounder a bit when I made rash decisions. Who knows?

If you have children, it is a natural instinct to take care of their problems, but this can cause long-term damage to children as they grow into adults. They do not understand there is a price to pay for their mistakes. Even though we help our children, they become adults and must learn to pay the cost for their own mistakes. As hard as it is, as I recently discussed with a client who has children now growing to adults, we have to learn to let those we love fail. If we try to influence them into what we see they need to become—instead of letting them make their own decisions and pay the price for poor decisions—they can begin to view us as a crutch. And then one day they are on their own and cannot navigate through the failures they will face.

> *Parents need to be their kids' leaders, not their friends. Your job as a parent is not to be liked. It's to help your kids become healthy, functioning adults.*

> —AUTHOR UNKNOWN

The truth is, I often stepped out of the box and did things without consulting others. Doing things my own way seemed like a no-brainer—which is often exactly what it was.

Looking back on my life, I have come to see that the actions I took were frequently simply to prove someone wrong and to prove myself right. Yes, that's how big my ego was. Being told I couldn't or shouldn't do something unfailingly propelled me to do it. For me, the most important thing always was to be viewed as a winner. I believe that this ego-driven flaw is what made my future chaos so unbearable; my failure could not be hidden from others. Rather, it was a revelation that I was less than perfect, that I was not always a winner. It was a bitter pill to swallow.

> *But the worst enemy you can meet will always be yourself; you lie in wait for yourself in caverns and forests. Lonely one, you are going the way to yourself! And your way goes past yourself, and past your seven devils! You will be a heretic to yourself and witch and soothsayer and fool and doubter and unholy one and villain. You must be ready to burn yourself in your own flame: how could you become new, if you had not first become ashes?*

> —Friedrich Nietzsche

There were more jobs, and there were more episodes of losing jobs. No matter where I worked, something about my attitude, my failure to cooperate with supervision, kept coming up. I was very good at what I did, but I was also very independent. I never wanted to play by the rules. I always wanted to be in the front, and I had a very big problem—I was constitutionally unable to take a hard look in the mirror and realize how often I was my own worst enemy. In Greek drama, it's called hubris, the excessive pride that often leads one to catastrophe. Fortunately, or otherwise, as life went on I always had someone to bail me out when I went over the line, so I never had to face the brutal facts about myself, which meant I never had to change.

On the positive side, hard work and long hours did not bother me. I can remember very few times in my adult life that I did not work two jobs simultaneously. Overtime was a blessing because it gave me the extra money I needed to do what I always seemed to do—live beyond my means. With my mother as a reliable safety net, I always had someone who would bail me out if needed.

When the company where I was working fell on hard times and cut our hours to twenty-eight hours a week, I turned to collecting scrap metal to support my family. It was pretty lucrative and helped us through the gas crisis of 1973. I also went into the lawn care business for a few years and networked my services to owners of rental property. This, too, sustained us with supplemental income for a few years. And I sold printing for a friend of mine who had opened his own print shop.

These sideline businesses instilled in me the desire to be my own boss. It was what I wanted; it was where I wanted to go. It seemed that if I was to discover a way to become self-employed, to be my own boss, that my life would be complete.

My desire to work regardless of my situation got me through those days. It might have been a lot easier if I had ever considered the idea of a budget. The idea of saving for a rainy day was a totally foreign concept. It was just too easy, even in those days, to obtain credit cards and run up balances. It was fairly easy to get by just making those minimum payments.

Whatever it took to get by—long hours, multiple jobs— was not a problem. My role was to support the family I had started. However, even at that young age, I had already over obligated myself financially. And it was beginning to hurt.

To be honest, I never remember a time in my life when I was not under the gun financially. Credit cards were always part of the issue. I mean, you could charge thousands of dollars a month and the minimum monthly charge was only about twenty dollars. It was an irresistible way for a young, headstrong, ambitious guy to get what he wanted without waiting.

To sensible men, every day is a day of reckoning.

—JOHN W. GARDNER

4

The Direction Of Self-Employment

Self-employment isn't a career choice; it is a lifestyle choice.

—Author unknown

Over the years, working countless hours in multiple jobs, several things were becoming apparent:

1. Hard work did not bother me.
2. I was not a good employee.
3. I hated supervision and supervisors.

I needed to make my own path, which was made a lot easier since I always had a safety net to provide an escape route.

So I continued to live above my means, work multiple jobs and long hours, and increasingly rely on credit to cushion our finances.

It's clear to me now that through this period of my life I was not establishing the family relations I should have had. As we age and look back over our years as young adults and young parents, often we see where we were not all we could have been to the very important people in our lives, people that depended upon us, not just for the necessities of life, but also for the inner strength each had to develop to become beneficial members of society. Even though I had my family at a very young age, it does make me wonder what would have been different if I had built a career and business before launching a family. Though this hindsight offers unique insight and wisdom, it often is not present at the time we so often need it. If you are like I used to be, seeking the counsel of mentors simply is not an option to consider.

Then, one evening as I was working my main job running a printing press, I happened to see a *Mother Earth News* magazine with an article called "Become a Chimney Sweep" by a company called August West. That article opened me to the world of chimney sweeps and how there was a growing need for their services in America due to the energy crisis of the seventies, which had resulted in gas shortages and rising fuel costs. This magazine grabbed my full attention—maybe this was it, maybe this was the moment of opportunity that I had been looking for.

Here was a business, they claimed, I could enter for $1,895 for everything I would need, including a top hat (I mean, you had to have a top hat, right?). I already had a '74 GMC window van. I could simply remove the seats and put a ladder rack on it. So I immediately sent off for the information and received it a few days later.

I did some research and discovered there was only one guy in my area sweeping chimneys. People were hiring him and paying him forty-five dollars each to sweep their chimneys! I thought this was divine providence for sure. I was never intended to work for others. I had proven that many times over the years. And suddenly, here was an escape route—a full-time way to be self-employed with a very low barrier to entry and lots of potential.

Once again I used my reliable safety net to get started. I still remember the look on my parent's faces when I told them I wanted to be a chimney sweep. One of the things I had to tell them was exactly what a chimney sweep was. But again, bless her generous heart, my mother supported me, and we went to the bank to borrow $2,500. It was my first business loan (which I only got because she agreed to cosign the note. What a lady!)

Fortunately, August West was running a sale on everything (complete with top hat) for $1,599. In my infinite wisdom, I figured I could borrow $2,500 for the money to buy the equipment and still have the operating funds I needed to go into business. Perfect.

I outfitted my first van just like the photos in the literature. When my equipment arrived, it was a simple matter of putting the stuff in the van and I was on my way.

It was too late to get listed in the yellow pages. This was prior to the Internet, and in that time frame a service business lived and died by the yellow pages. That may be hard to fathom in this day of the mobile device and the amazing research vehicle we call Google, where we can reach prospects and where people find us today. So I ran an ad in the local newspaper. It was a one-inch-column ad that ran daily in its service directory and cost me sixty dollars a month. I later found out that it's a great idea to advertise on the obituary page because *everybody* looks at that page in a small southern town!

My loan proceeds quickly dwindled away. I had gotten a phone line, opened a checking account, and had even bought insurance. My liability insurance premium for the year was seventy-seven dollars! And the chimney sweeping kit from the supplier, while containing a lot of things, sure did not provide all the things needed.

When the ad was published, my phone started ringing off the hook. Before I knew it, my new business had been launched from that simple one-inch classified ad.

I also began to do network marketing, though I didn't know it was called that back then. I went to the stores in town that sold wood stoves, hoping they would give me leads. One day when I went in the Englander Stove Store in Concord, Roy, the owner, told me, "I am tired of working with the public. I want out." So being true to my impulsive nature, I asked what he wanted for the business. He said he'd take $5,000 for everything. I said, "It's a deal." And that was the launch of my retail career.

Now, understand, I was still working a full-time job on the night shift of a local printing company, running a chimney service business, and as if that wasn't enough, I had entered the retail business. The only solution I could think of to handle the additional work was to utilize my unemployed wife to run the store. After all, the kids were all in school, and if we could locate the store near the house, the kids could be taken care of and we could run the business. Since I worked at night and my workweek was four days a week, I thought that we could do this.

So without having the money, I committed. I figured by the time we closed the deal, I would be able to come up with the $5,000. I was taking hardly any money out of the chimney sweeping business, and by this time, I was savvy enough to have begun building some reserves. That first fall as a chimney sweep, I worked my night shift job Monday through Thursday and spent each day, until early afternoon, doing chimneys. By only working a four-day workweek, I had all day on Friday and Saturday to also work in the chimney business. It was physically taxing and at times grueling, but it was doable.

Did we have a business plan? Nope. We did it simply by the seat of our pants. Looking back today as a coach, I wonder what a coach would have said about what I was doing? It would have likely given him some great stories to share with his coaching buddies about this crazy dude running a service business who then opened a retail location all while still working a full-time job. To be honest, in those days my thoughts ran in cycles of the bills we had. I well remember the months when we were on easy street, when there were five paychecks in a month (we got paid every week). When I first computed my income, I based it on the five-week months, but there are only four months each year with five paydays. This was how the boat deal happened; it wasn't until later that I realized this would make the other eight months of the year tough.

We needed a location for our new retail enterprise. I searched and found a barbershop near our house that had just been bought by a friend who was going to build a used car lot on the property. I asked about renting the little building, and he agreed to it. We committed to remodeling the building, and he rented it to me for $125 a month.

We began getting the barbershop up and running as a wood stove store. Just so you get the idea, this building was a one-chair barbershop. It did not have a lot of room, to say the least. Nevertheless, we moved into it and were now in the chimney sweep *and* the woodstove business—all without a speck of business training between us. Our storage space was really just shelves in the restroom, and it was not a large restroom!

I had no idea what a budget was. I had no idea what a margin was. I had no clue how to price things. For some reason, I had never even thought about profit or cash reserves. I was the classic case of a guy running his business from a checking account, who would buy stuff and hoped to sell it before payments under the thirty-day terms were due. So I asked the former owner how much to mark up a wood stove. He told me $200. Without any further consideration, I followed this advice. I didn't bother to calculate what had to come out of that $200 markup—I had no idea how to do that. I soon found out it had to cover paying the freight on each stove, paying the rent, and paying all the other costs of doing business. It doesn't take a business genius to see that the markup didn't leave a lot left over. But that's what I did, at least until I discovered more about the financial realities of running a retail business.

The following spring another opportunity presented itself. The owner of Wood Energy Systems, another hearth shop in town, told me he was closing. If I was interested, I could move into his building. I figured this was a good move. It had a lot more room, and the location was established. So we moved to our new location. I was still balancing the full-time job, the chimney sweep service, the retail business—the whole shebang.

Since I was suddenly self-employed, I began to really bridle under the pressure of my night job. One night, due mostly to a dislike of my direct supervisor, I decided I was done. The next day I walked into the office and told the plant manager I was quitting, effective immediately. I did not say it in so many words, but in the back of my head I heard that song "Take This Job and Shove It." I remember thinking as I left the plant after that abrupt resignation that now the world was going to see all I would accomplish as an entrepreneur. Yep. It was how the free enterprise system worked, and I was going to be a star.

When I quit my printing job in April, I was oblivious to the fact that chimney cleaning was not going to attract customers in the spring and summer. Guess I hadn't bothered to ask about that. But somehow we managed to make it through that first summer. However, it was pretty much pure luck. Not only did I still not know much at all about business, but also I did not realize even then how little I knew about the chimney business.

I am amazed by the good luck I had back then to avoid burning down a bunch of houses. As it turned out, there is a whole lot to know about chimneys, fireplaces, woodstoves, furnaces, etc., and none of that was part of my very cursory initial training. I truly had no idea what in the world I was doing. In short, I didn't know what I didn't know.

Over the summer months that year I started to get mailings from August West, the company I had bought my chimney sweeping equipment from. I found there was some type of testing being offered for chimney sweeps at the University of North Carolina. This was a test to certify woodstove installers. Miraculously, I passed that test and suddenly held my first certification. Over the years, this evolved into what is now known as certification by the National Fireplace Institute. Little did I know that one day I would be the certification chair of this organization!

But the most important thing that happened that day was getting to meet other chimney sweeps. Some of them already knew each other. They invited me to lunch, and one of them, a sweep who was an officer with the National Chimney Sweep Guild, told me about an upcoming meeting in Hendersonville I should attend. It was a meeting of the North Carolina Guild of Professional Chimney Sweeps. My wife and I decided to go.

With almost zero understanding of what it was all about, we headed to Hendersonville early on a Saturday morning. We didn't even have room reservations. We managed to locate the Holiday Inn where the meeting would be held. I went inside and discovered it had a hot tub. I went back out to the parking lot and told my wife we were staying. They had a hot tub! To this day I wonder if that hot tub was the beginning of something. I know if it had not been there, I might not have stayed. Funny how a little thing like a hot tub can change your life!

5

Life Changes

After checking into the meeting and paying the fee, I found that this was a hotel full of chimney sweeps from all over the southeast. As I sat through those classes, I discovered there was a lot more to this than I ever imagined. I quickly realized that building relationships with these people would be the way for me to move forward.

Perhaps the most influential person I met at that meeting was a guy named Pete Luter. He had a similar business to mine and was already well established in the industry. He also had an Afro-style haircut that said a lot about his occasional in-your-face persona. We developed a strong friendship, which, while rocky at times because of our strong individual personalities, endured for many years. Pete has since departed this world, but the things I learned from him about this industry still are with me. He was one of the most innovative thinkers I ever met. He knew a lot about all kinds of things. Any conversation with him was always informative and interesting. He left his mark on the chimney industry as one of the first exceptional teachers. He was, in fact, hugely instrumental in developing the National Chimney Sweep Training School near Indianapolis. His commitment to the industry was an inspiration to me. To put it simply, he was the template for the person I wanted to be in the industry. He was an icon. I knew I could learn a lot just by hanging out with him.

As a result, I served in the industry in many capacities in the following years, both through trade associations and educational foundations. It is a great source of pride that I have likely held more volunteer leadership positions than any other person in the chimney and venting industry. I continued building my strength in the industry and my knowledge of all things related to fireplaces, venting, and all associated structures and appliances. Eventually, these strengths laid the foundation for a coaching career I would develop many years later.

Another influential person with whom I developed a very close relationship was Roger Charon. He was somewhat of a brother but more of a father to me and shared with me inspirational thoughts when I needed them. Roger has also passed from this world, but I often think of Roger and the advice he gave me. One of his most inspirational sayings of all came after he saw me arguing with another person. "Never argue with an idiot; from across the street, no one can tell who the idiot is," he said. I often share this phrase today, sharing it with others when they see themselves tempted to engage in a senseless argument.

But I'm getting ahead of myself. My coaching career happened well after the day the chaos arrived!

6

Fitting Into An Industry

Focus on building the best possible business. If you are great, people will notice, and opportunities will appear.

—Mark Cuban

Returning home, my first wife and I began to build our retail business to new levels. That was the cornerstone of everything else we accomplished. We simultaneously grew our service business. These efforts resulted in two relocations of the retail operation and the service business.

Initially, the business operated from our home. Then we moved to a small one-chair barbershop building, and over the history of my business growth, we relocated to a retail location with about 800 square feet, then to a 2,000-square-foot location in a strip mall shopping center, and finally arrived at our own building of 12,500 square feet. Later, as we entered manufacturing, we utilized more locations, at one point operating out of two locations simultaneously, one for the retail/service businesses and the other for the manufacturing that was to come in later years.

However, also during this time my first wife and I divorced. I married my second wife, Sheryl, who immediately became and remains a solid basis of support for me—a true rock. Sheryl is my spouse, my soul mate, and my best friend. Sometimes you just know a person is the one you are supposed to share life with. Such is the relationship we have. And as the chaos descended, it was a good thing to have her by my side. I'm convinced I would have never survived it without her steadfast and remarkable support.

During this period I built a sizable chimney service business. We offered services beyond simple chimney sweeping. We added chimney repair and air duct cleaning as well. We even became one of the largest chimney relining contractors in the country. This—together with my status as president of national trade associations and national industry educational foundations and my involvement in other state and national trade groups and certifying agencies—made me quite prominent in the industry. It was a very gratifying time.

One of the things that affected my career and my business at this time was *The E-Myth* by Michael Gerber. This book taught me so much, and it has affected so many others and given them business acumen. The premise of *The E-Myth* is to build the replicatable business, a business built on systems, a business built where one can have the freedom wished for, which is one of the reasons why so many of us start our own enterprises, even though we often become prisoners of our businesses and of our shattered dreams. So along with building the business, I also started to assemble a set of standard operating systems that I have shared with many others. The teachings of *The E-Myth* are, I believe, one of the guiding lights for the small-business owner to move to the level sought.

> *Go to work on your business, not in it.*
>
> —Michael Gerber

Even as I write this book Gerber remains an influence on me today. Earlier today I received a video from him talking of the word legacy and the legacy he wants to leave with his fellow-man, and it inspired me to think about my own legacy and even pass along in a social post this question: What is the legacy you will leave with another? You see, one of the major purposes of this book is not to create a sense of sorrow for the things I have undergone in my own life, but rather to open others' eyes and inspire them to the true greatness that exists in them. If this occurs, then my mission with this book has been realized.

On the retail side, we had gone from a tiny showroom showing a couple of woodstoves to a full-line fireplace shop. Then we added patio furnishings. We even gained prominence as one of the first companies on the East Coast to offer outdoor living products such as grilling islands, outdoor fireplaces, outdoor furniture, and other products to enrich the leisure time of homeowners. Eventually, we were featured on the cover of industry publications, articles were written about what we were doing in industry trade journals and these portrayed our operation as one of innovative thinking and we were viewed as industry pioneers.

It was at this juncture we befriended Ken Warren. We had known him from the industry for many years but never had developed a relationship with him. He functioned as a sales manager for our new manufacturing entity. This guy knew more about how to take product to market than anyone I had ever met. He was a genius. But more important was the relationship we built with Ken as a mentor and a friend whose support we would come to rely on when the chaos hit the fan. Like Roger Charon had been in my earlier life, Ken became a person whom I could depend upon, and who was there when I needed a friend. As I develop my skills in the world of coaching, I try to return the gifts he gave to me by sharing with him tools to provide him the strength to continue striving to realize and live his dreams.

> *Good friends are like stars. You don't always see them, but you know they're always there.*

> —AUTHOR UNKNOWN

In the process, I was also building a solid résumé as an industry expert, something that would serve me well later, when the chaos arrived. Gradually I began to have a profound effect on the industry and the people in it. This was not always a smooth process. I'm sure some people thought I was an opinionated jerk. They were probably right, but I am who I am. Although I ruffled feathers along the way, I am hopeful I helped a fledgling industry become a strong and source of professional pride for many.

During these years I was requested to do speaking presentations. These turned out to be magical moments for me. It was then that I discovered teaching was something I wanted to do—a lot. It was hugely rewarding, and it was a natural for me. It was in my sweet spot. Without ever looking for it, I had found a whole new niche for myself. I loved it. And like so many other skills I picked up at that time, it would serve me very well in the future.

Around that time it also became evident that my parents were aging. I had two sets of parents because my father and mother had divorced when I was very young. I don't recall ever living with my father and mother in the same house. I was four or five when they divorced. My memories of family times from this era are foggy. Growing up, I lived with my mother and my stepfather. I also spent limited time with my father and my stepmother. So, in one way or another, I now felt responsible for all of them. As we entered the new century, my parents started to accept that they would increasingly need to rely on someone else for their care and their decisions. Since there were no other relatives to rely on, their care fell on my shoulders—a responsibility Sheryl and I simply accepted. That alone says a lot about her amazing character and commitment.

It was during these times that I made an amazing discovery: the "credit line." This was an amount of money you could draw upon at any time, with the bank just waiting for you to call for some. Need $25,000? Not a problem; you just called the bank and requested them to transfer the money to your checking account. You could get any amount of money you wanted; you just had to guarantee it. This meant that even though you could get the money at a moment's notice, it was not simply a gift. You pledged material items to guarantee it—things like your savings account, the available value of your home above the mortgage amount, or anything else of value to guarantee the bank would be paid. All of a sudden we had hundreds of thousands of dollars we could put our hands on at any time.

We had more funds available to us through the credit card companies, and there was a high number of credit cards with available cash that was so easy to get. I think at one time I could easily have gotten my hands on three-quarters of a million dollars within a few hours.

We began to make arrangements for my parents. Houses were sold, and new homes were bought. One was built. My mother and stepfather ended up living with us. We built a house down the street for my father and stepmother. We hired a full-time caregiver to assist each set of parents with cooking, laundry, and housekeeping. We did our best to maintain the most private life we could for three different families, each one part of my extended family. A part of this was the signing of living wills and finding out what each person in our care wanted in case a decision as to that person's care needed to be made. We also managed the financial affairs of all of them. Sheryl was juggling quite a few checking accounts at one time to cover all the needs of business, our personal lives, and my parents' lives, all the checks a different color and when she wrote out checks it looked like all the colors of the rainbow spread out on her desk.

As our parents age, the roles reverse. From childhood, your parents raise you, there comes the day you leave the nest and go to make your own way in the world. But there comes a time in your life that your parents start to need you, much as you need them when you are a child. This is where the child now becomes the patriarch of the family, or the child chooses to ignore the needs of the parents. Our choice was to become the parents to my parents who, due to their declining health, are no longer able to make decisions for themselves. This can be a blessing to some, or to others a curse, but to us, it was how we felt we had to look after the people who had looked after me.

But life can deal cruel blows. My mother, the support and safety net who had always been there for me, went into a rapid health decline with heart issues and strokes and ended up passing away on New Year's Eve in 2001. This was made even more difficult because I was the one who had to decide to discontinue her life support system. If you have ever sat and held the hand and said goodbye to a person who is a part of your life, you understand that it is one of the most humbling experiences you can ever undergo. It is when you realize just how unimportant you are in the universe. Without a vision and hope of a higher power, it is hard to navigate through these moments of our lives. Although I was acting according to her wishes, it is not a task I would wish on anyone. It also just happened that New Year's Eve was the anniversary of my marriage to Sheryl.

> *You never get over the death of your mother; you simply learn to live with it.*

> —Author unknown

At the time of the writing of this book, my parents and step-parents have all passed away. It is only in the last few short years that Sheryl and I have not had to look after parents or deal with assisted living centers, hospital rooms, hospice, and bedside death.

All of these things are part of life. Ultimately they make us stronger and more appreciative of what we have, but while we're dealing with them, they are not easy to endure. Afterward, we cannot help but feel somewhat guilty that we didn't use more of our parents' time with us to engage with them in more meaningful ways. I suppose everyone has these regrets when their parents move on, but that knowledge doesn't make it any less heart-wrenching in the end.

Soon, all our businesses were prospering. The outdoor living initiative moved us to a new level in 2004. *Hearth & Home Magazine* wrote a story about us and featured Sheryl and me on the cover. We were established as leaders in the outdoor living industry. We were consulted as experts. We spoke on the subject. We trained others how to go after this market. We were featured in other industry magazines. We even began presenting seminars on outdoor living for trade groups and others in the industry.

It is an important part of my story to note that along the way we had learned the value and ease of lines of credit. Remember, credit was so easy to get back then. Credit cards with $100,000 credit limits very easy to procure. Banks were eager to lend money. So we followed the same path as many other business owners. We lived lavishly, we appeared rich, and we looked flush, but in actuality, all of it was based on credit. It was an illusion. Like so many others, we fell prey to the lure of the easy and abundant money that was being offered everywhere. And that was a big mistake. It was one we would pay dearly for when chaos arrived. In fact, it was this mistake above all else that contributed to the chaos we and others had to endure when the financial world collapsed around us in 2008.

Hindsight is always twenty-twenty, but back then, with this credit so readily available, we found it easy to enter the world of manufacturing. We developed a proprietary means of building a product for the outdoor living world. Soon, once again, we were viewed as the industry leaders in this.

7

Funding: The Gift Horse From Above

How well I remember a conversation one night with my
friend and mentor Ken Warren. It was a late night drive
back from the Midwest and he asked me a question, one that
was never expected. He asked, "Jerry, how much business do
you want to do a month?" My answer was, "Ken, I want us to
do at least $250,000 a month, and I think we can build it to
$500,000." He then said something that was a reality check:
"Well, to do that you will need that much money in the bank
to back it."

Wow. That was a shocker. It seems so obvious now, but
back then I hadn't thought about it. When a business builds
product, it has to buy and pay for raw materials. It must pay
a workforce to turn those raw materials into a finished product. Eventually, you sell the product, often on thirty-day terms.
Well, to do all that you have to have the money up front to
cover those very real expenses.

It was that night it dawned on me that when I spent a
dollar, I may not get that dollar back for quite a while. But,

hey—so what. We were good, we were bank funded, and our bank had *plenty* of money to fund this. All we had to do was pay the interest.

Unfortunately, while we were building product and prototypes, the one thing we did not build was financial reserves. Quite frankly, given the climate of easy credit back then, we saw no need to. We were building an empire. We knew that once it was complete, we would be able to sell this empire to someone else and move along after pocketing a tidy profit.

We devoted hundreds of thousands of dollars to the development of this outdoor living product line. If I had an idea, I simply instructed my team to build it without even bothering to research if there was a need. There was never a thought for the budget or if there would be a return on the investment. Many of these bright ideas never paid off, and those failures were not cheap. We created a workable product and took it to market. Unfortunately, in the end, we just did not procure the required funding to do it correctly, we had bigger ideas than our finding would allow is to make it happen. We had every reason to believe the bank would provide this for us. But little did we know that just over the horizon a disaster that would obliterate all those plans was waiting to pounce on us.

Starting we built our product in a spare space in the warehouse of our retail operation, but we quickly moved into one and then another facility that was more suitable. Perhaps we were a bit cavalier with our investments back then. It's easy to see that now. But at the time it seemed like a great idea to be bold and seize the opportunity while we could. I'm sure others felt the same way about their opportunities back then. After all, the insidious undoing of the economy was under the radar of pretty much everyone. Even the Securities and Exchange Commission had failed to detect Wall Street's actions that were about to crash the economy. The sun of financial abundance was shining brightly. Little did we or anyone suspect that it was just the calm before the storm. The Bull was getting ready to crash head on into the wall!

So, build we did. We were eventually utilizing a total of almost forty thousand square feet of space between our manufacturing facility and our retail/sweep locations. We had a workforce of close to forty. Additionally, during this short time frame, the factory moved three times, we bought equipment, and we moved our executive offices from the retail location to the factory. Quite plainly during this period, manufacturing became our focus, and we took the eye off the ball that was producing the bread and butter were our retail/service operations. We had a vision of greatness and likely looked at it with rose-colored glasses when we should have been looking at making perhaps more sound decisions.

Looking back is easy, here was a successful enterprise, we took the profits from the solid side, and we devoted those to the side we were building, without a thought for the what ifs of the world, I mean we had a great idea and we knew it would work. But in the process, we took our eye off the other, not knowing that this would be a part of the kiss of death to our enterprises.

8

The Blinders Of Easy Funding

Given all that was going on, it was not hard to see how we could take our eyes off the ball a bit. We let our ambitions for the business get ahead of our very real financial constraints. We got a bit blinded by our desire to make things happen quickly, which probably led us to rely much too heavily on credit to fund ourselves. Way too heavily, in fact. Perhaps if we had only instituted sound budgeting principals, built a plan and stayed with it, but we were way to head strong.

We also learned another hard lesson. We failed to follow up on and consolidate the interest we were getting from dealers. We had large numbers of dealers interested in our products. We even offered free training once a month with as many as one hundred people in attendance. They came to our facility, we did classes, we served lots of meals, and we built piles of interest. But instead of working with the dealers whose interest we had already gained, we kept pursuing more and more dealers. That is an easy mistake to make when you are growing too fast, and it hurt us. Here are people interested, make it work for them, but instead we kept chasing more and more, even though we could have never supplied the demand if they all took off.

Adding insult to injury, I had taken my eye completely off my bread and butter, the chimney service and the fireplace and outdoor living center. Once I took my eye off that ball, it stopped rolling as it had for many years, delivering to me whatever I felt I needed or simply wanted.

> *Life is denied by lack of attention, whether it be to cleaning windows or trying to write a masterpiece.*
>
> —NADIA BOULANGER

9

Chaos Begins With A Vengeance

Now this is not the end, it is not even the beginning of the end. But it is, perhaps, the end of the beginning.

—WINSTON CHURCHILL

Things continued in this way until September 28, 2008, the day the stock market tumbled, the day the banks' pools of cash to lend began to evaporate. From that day forward, even banks could no longer borrow the money they needed. It seems that the banks, just like us, were living on borrowed money. Call it greed. Call it wrong. It doesn't matter. It was the way the world operated then. I simply call it *reality*.

The economy tanked. Just like that, it went south, totally south, like all the way to Antarctica. Without warning, we were facing what would be America's worst financial crisis since the Great Depression. But even at the outset, many of us felt (or hoped) it would just be a blip on the radar screen, just another short-lived crisis. After all, it had been decades since such a calamity had happened in America. For most of us, the Great Depression was simply a story we learned from our parents, something from their past that had nothing to do with our future.

Just a few days later, Congress put together a second package to bail us all out, and the package passed. Whew! Unfortunately, the damage was already done. It was only dimly that any of us could even fathom the tsunami that was coming next. Later would be the auto bailout, bank bailouts, and other rescues, but there was no life preserver being thrown to small businesses. We were floating on our own. Suddenly there were once again days when you wondered if the bread lines would be forming again as they did in the thirties during the Great Depression.

Beware of a wolf in sheep's clothing.

—AESOP

They called it the Troubled Assets Recovery Program, better known as TARP. "Troubled assets"—it had a comfortable ring to it, though it didn't begin to describe the seriousness of the problem or just whose assets were actually in trouble. This bill was promoted as the bill to save the banks that were *too big to fail.* All of this is written in many different accounts. Whatever the form, it's always ugly. But this story, my story, is what this day of chaos did to me and, I'm sure, multitudes of other Americans. But it was mostly to the owners of businesses that, like mine, had been built and grown on what seemed like the solid foundation of limitless credit. And of course, on a lot of sweat, blood, and tears as well!

It quickly became evident that many others, like me, had operated on the principle of equity lending. That ended abruptly when the Federal Deposit Insurance Corporation and the Federal Reserve System decided this had to change. The banking environment of the time was commonly called *toxic*. And it was. But this is not the story of toxic loans. This is the story of how those toxic loans, in the flash of an eye, simply expunged the businesses, homes, and life savings of many hard-working business owners. The result? Many people like me had to start over from scratch. Everything we had labored to build for so many years was simply liquidated. This is what chaos is all about, and this was the reward, of ourselves and many others, for playing the easy-credit game. We lost, as did some of the banks. Many business owners who had worked their tails off for years lost their businesses, their homes, and their savings. It was a terrible time for many, often viewed as being as catastrophic as the Great Depression of the 1930s.

But this is not a book about the sorrow of the times. Rather, it is a book of how chaos reinvented a guy who exemplified the classic crash and failure of those harsh times. My goal is not to depress you, rather my goal is to excite you as to what can happen, so please read on, I write this as a path for you, not to shed tears for me. But my goal is also to impart how important proper budgeting and business planning is to keep from falling over the cliff, once you fall over the cliff that is an extremely hard climb back. The bruises stay with you for a really long time.

The effect of that day was felt far and wide. Credit simply dried up. To make matters far worse, the banks were practically rabid to recover any and all assets, most especially the loans they had made, what the banking industry called "the paper" this being the loan agreements made with people like myself. This panic by the banks to forestall their own failure destroyed many businesses, caused massive layoffs and crippled the world economy. Huge institutions, like Lehman Brothers, unimaginably went under. Large banks were absorbed by others, community banks failed and bank consolidations became the common news of the day. Everyone was scrambling to stem the tide of damage. The common news stories of the day centered on yet another toxic bank and more bank failures, we commonly heard that banks could not pass a stress test, and this meant they could not survive if loans defaulted. And this is our story.

As I said, the bank bailout did finally get voted on and approved by the Congress and rapidly signed into law by the president. Many of us really had no idea of the true significance of this. The facts only gradually came to light over the ensuing years. But what we witnessed was the failure of banks, some were large and also the small ones started to fold up and be absorbed by others, maybe a better word would be consumed by others. All over America, small and large business owners started to see their credit lines being called in. Credit lines often secured by the owner's home, his life savings, his insurance policies and his retirement funds. Talk about a reward for the blood, sweat, tears and sacrifices so many had made!

Now some of the larger businesses, General Motors in the auto industry for one, were saved as the government came to their aid. But for multitudes of small-business owners, there was not government assistance. Quite frankly, we were on our own, even though small business employs more workers in the United States than the large companies like General Motors and Chrysler. We were left to flounder on our own.

If you have never been self-employed, you may not understand how a business is financed. The vast majority of businesses prior to 2008 had open lines of credit with their banks. This was their operating capital, and many of us had been taught that this was simply how business was conducted. Yes, we may have heard some talk of cash reserves, and the banking of cash, but did we listen? Of course not. It was simply too easy to obtain our bank funding, and when it ran low we just went and got some more. And the banks were eager to give it to us.

Business, of course, produces a product or a service and then resells it. However, from the time that process begins until an invoice is paid, there is a need for cash to run the business. This is often a considerable amount of money. This money also costs money in the form of interest. It's considered part of the cost of doing business because funding is required to provide the cash for day-to-day operations. After all, your employees want to be paid every payday, and your suppliers do not want to wait until you are paid for them to get paid.

The whole idea of a credit line is that it is not to be used as a long-term loan. In fact, it is supposed to be paid off at least once a year for a period of thirty days. Banks make money by lending money with interest. It is not uncommon for a bank to borrow money from the government simply to loan to others, like me. The bank makes income on this loan because the government loans it to the bank at an interest rate well below what the bank charges us, its customers. During the boom years, the banks let the rules slide.

Even though you were supposed to clear the loan for thirty days once a year, very few did. That meant you could let the loan continue without paying it off. And that was a dangerous thing to allow because it gave the appearance that it wasn't necessary to be really on top of those payments. Those credit lines came to be viewed as the ongoing (as in never-ending) funding that existed to support way too many small businesses.

Naturally, after the crash in 2008, as business slowed drastically, so did the flow of money. Since there was a slowdown of money, the entire system was quickly getting out of whack. Money is not always in someone's hands or in the bank; a phenomenal sum of money is always in the hands of others or is tied up with noncash assets. It could be a check in the mail. It could be an invoice waiting to be paid or simply inventory sitting on a shelf somewhere. Because of payment delays, slow payers and other traps for cash, often a business needs money from other sources to operate. Those other sources were often bank lenders.

Some years earlier, we had learned how to leverage ourselves with loans. All it took was paperwork filed with the bank showing something called your GCF, which stands for global cash flow. With the right GCF and with property as collateral (even property with a mortgage but some appreciable cash value), you could qualify for a loan. The banks were glad to do this. It was how they made money. Even more to their advantage was the fact they were insured in case of failure. However, by subscribing to this insurance, the banks also were placed under the power of the Federal Deposit Insurance Corporation, and it, in effect, is ruled by the Federal Reserve System. Without their continued support, no bank could operate.

This is all just basic economics. We had three separate business initiatives divided among several corporations. And like other businesses, we had credit lines that were funding each of those businesses. Credit lines such as these must be "guaranteed" by the business owners—in this case, *me*! That guarantee was something I never fully understood when I signed those loan documents. I never even read what I was signing. Do you ever stop and read all that fine print when you sign for a loan, probably not, how well I remember signing some pages and initialing others, not ever aware that you may be painting a big target right over your forehead.

Why should I have just signed these loan documents? The banks were our friends. They were how we grew our business, and business was good, very good. We were continuing to produce product and to spend money marketing our product to support our overhead. We just signed on the dotted line, took our cash, and went on our merry way. It never occurred to me for a minute that what I was doing was putting a big noose around my neck and the floor beneath me was beginning to shift. I was building on very shaky ground! Or perhaps it was more like quicksand as you don't fall all at once, it is more of a slow continuous sinking into the depths of despair.

2008 was an election year. Because of this, many of us concluded that once the election was behind us, the economy would stabilize and things would improve. So much for that notion. The election came and went, and the economy did not change a bit, the downward spiral continued, and seemed to pick up speed, dropping faster and faster! The noose began tightening. Since nothing changed with the election, we pinned our hopes on the end of the year. I mean, don't manufacturing sales and demand for product always accelerate again in January? But January 1, 2009, came and went, and we saw no relief. Life all over America had a cloud over it.

We were making really innovative products: outdoor living cabinetry, outdoor kitchens, fire pits, fireplaces, and wood-fired pizza oven housings. Our proprietary methods were radically innovative and unlike anything else; we had built the proverbial better mousetrap. The bankers even said we were moving in the direction to really own the outdoor living market in America. One of our bankers even talked of investing personally but realized that would have been a violation of the banking laws. (We were soon to discover all we could ever want to know about banking laws).

At any rate, we thought we had it all figured out. The bank was assuring us *it* had it all figured out for us also. We would have our operating capital and our loans for increased funding renewed soon. Not to worry.

Our credit lines at the time were due to expire in April of 2009. Not a problem. We knew our banks would provide financial sustenance, as it always had. So we continued to plow ahead, ready to make it all happen in 2009. We were absolutely certain this whole mess was going to clear up at any moment. I mean, this was America, the greatest country in the world. No way was our economy going to get worse. That's what we told ourselves. Loan officers assured and encouraged us: "Don't worry; it is just taking us a little longer to process loans now than before. It's all good." I don't know who was more delusional, the banks or ourselves. But soon we noticed houses were no longer being built in the same numbers. In fact, it looked like construction was actually halting! Impossible! We had been in a bull market for so long. Still, we remained confident.

So, lulled into this false sense of security, we put our heads in the sand and continued to ignore the signs that were becoming clearer and clearer. It certainly helped our willingness to be deluded that during this time, we were able to secure some short-term loans for $100,000 each, but these loans were simply another bridge to the disaster that was going to come. Clearly, to us, the banks were going to be there for us. We fully believed we were going to sign that big package at any time. We simply knew it. I mean what other choice did the banks have, they certainly could not afford for us to fail! Or could they?

Seek the truth or hide your head in the sand. Both require digging.

—ANDREW NOLAN

10

The Storm Clouds Build

However, as we approached April 2009, our credit lines were not being renewed. One banker continued to assure us. "We are working on it," he said over and over. But we were beginning to feel very uncomfortable. Perhaps, finally, we were becoming really aware of the massive disruption that was lying in wait for us just down the road.

We even sought a private equity company. We felt that it might be a possible alternative that could save our bacon if the banks didn't come through. The private equity firm's source of money was insurance companies and others with large cash reserves who wanted to get a better return on their cash than the stock market or banks could deliver. It seemed promising. But it all turned into dead ends, very dead ends. It seemed even the private equity firms were retreating into their shells like frightened turtles.

It is important to realize that at this point we had two homes—one we lived in and one I had built for my father and stepmother. We ended up with the mortgage payments on both houses when my parents moved to assisted living because of declining health. We knew we only needed one. We put both houses on the market, figuring we would sell one and keep the other to live in. We even moved from the larger house to the other smaller one since it was originally planned as our own retirement home.

In fall 2009, both houses were on the market. The economy by that time had gotten very shaky. The funds we needed to run our businesses were evaporating like water in a desert. We knew there were several possible saving remedies, including selling one of the homes or finally getting the bank funding. We set our dwindling hopes on one of those coming to fruition. But we were not seeing activity on the real estate, nor were we seeing any signs of progress at the bank. The dark clouds of impending chaos were gathering, and we felt helpless to do anything about it.

Suddenly, in November of 2009, we saw a ray of hope. One of the houses was being shown, and the people looking at it wanted to buy it. We thought our prayers had been answered. Our real estate agent wanted us to come to the house we had moved out of. He had a buyer who had some questions. We went and met with a couple from another state. They said they wanted to rent the house for ten weeks. Following that, they had a deal closing and would pay us our asking price in cash. This appeared to be the lifeline we had been needing. They wanted to move in immediately. We signed the contracts that evening. Did it all sound a little too good to be true? Sure it did, but in our desperation, we overlooked that, like the fine print of the loans I had signed for years, and we plowed ahead.

Saturday afternoon they pulled into the driveway in a motor home. The value of that vehicle was several hundred thousand dollars. It was towing a large enclosed trailer. They wrote a check for one month's deposit and one month's rent. They took occupancy of the house that afternoon.

We had a check and they had a house. We were floating on air. This was the cash we needed to clear up our credit lines. We were going to be OK. At least we believed that was the case for a fleeting moment. Monday the check was deposited. Everything was going to be fine. Then Thursday came and the bank called and said the check was returned due to insufficient funds. It had bounced! Talk about an emotional seesaw! Once again, at the last minute, our hopes were dashed.

Now we had an even bigger problem. We had to evict them. It took over a month to get them out. By the time we finally managed to do that, the house had been severely damaged. What had looked for a moment like salvation had turned into just another crushing blow to our already fragile finances and hopes.

It seems the guy who had rented the house was a fugitive from an adjoining state. He was arrested at the house. When the eviction hearing was held, he was in jail. The couple was evicted. The amount of the check made his crime a felony. Fortunately, he had to make our check good or he would have gone to prison. And we got a house back that now needed quite a bit of repair!

We were, of course, still working with the bank. The way the lines of credit were set up, I was personally responsible for the money. Sheryl was not. The business had belonged to me, and we had a prenuptial agreement that exempted her from ownership *and* liability. All of this had been set up prior to our marriage to protect us in the event of divorce. Little did we know that the agreement would be one of the few saving graces in a very dark period of our lives.

During the month of December, we continued to negotiate with the bank for funding. Finally, we had a deal ready to go. The loan papers were forwarded to our attorney, and the closing date was set for the week of Christmas. The morning of the closing we got a call from our attorney. He had been instructed by the bank NOT to close the loan. The bank said it had to make "some changes to the paperwork."

A new date for signing was never set, and time was expiring. Our credit lines had not been renewed. We had been stretched out for months waiting on the bank to renew them but were always told things were taking a little longer. All banks were now tightening credit like a hangman's noose. Other business owners shared similar issues. Then the final straw was added. On January 4, 2010, my secretary went to the bank to make a payment on our homes and on the credit line. When she got back to the office, she told Sheryl that she did not know why, but the bank had left the checks for the house payment, building loan payment and credit line payment in the bag.

Thinking this had been a mistake, I told her to give me the checks, and I headed to the bank. When I got there, I walked up to the teller and slid several checks across the counter. She looked at them and the paperwork and punched some numbers into her computer. Then came the words that rocked my world: "Mr. Isenhour, I don't understand why, but I am being told I cannot accept your payments."

This, as you might imagine, was more than a little alarming. I asked her why not and she said, "Let me get Mr. Banker." Mr. Banker had been my banker for a lot of years. I saw her speak to him behind his desk, and his eyes got very large. He had a look of surprise on his face. He came to the door of his office and motioned for me. Once in his office, he said, "Jerry, I don't know what is wrong, but it says we need to contact the credit department." I told him to give them a call. He did, and he turned to me and said, "They want you to come to their office." I said, "Sure, I can be there in thirty minutes." Nope. That wasn't going to work. He simply told me they would be "in touch with me." It sounded pretty serious. After all, Mr. Banker had been my friend, my mentor, my confidant, but he had a worried look I had never seen him display before, an ominous look!

The only thing more shocking than the truth are the lies people tell to cover it up.

—AUTHOR UNKNOWN

Now we were really in a quandary. I had no idea what was going on or what to do. When I returned to my office, I contacted my attorney. His instructions were to make the payments via a transfer on the Internet. This we did. However, the next day the bank redeposited the money to our accounts, in effect refusing the payments.

At this point, we were out of ideas about how to proceed. In our contacts with Mr. Banker, which were often, I was simply told the credit department would be in touch with me. This went on for the next few weeks until January 25. That was the day the world really started to cave in, the day all possible escape routes were finally and completely blocked.

11

The Mail Arrives, With My Details Of A Financial Funeral

In our mailbox was a large stack of envelopes from the bank. They were letters of demand. The bank, without warning of any kind despite my years as its customer, had called every loan we had from it, both personal and business. It was unimaginable. But there it was in black and white; the whole ugly truth of our situation really hit us. The bank was calling every single one of our loans—mortgages, auto loans, credit lines, and the entire loan portfolio under my name. It meant we had to come up with the cash to repay every single bank loan in full, and we only had a few days to do it. If we couldn't comply, the bank would start foreclosure and repossession proceedings against us. It was that simple.

Now remember, the impetus for this state of affairs was that the bank had allowed the credit line to expire the previous April, even though it continued to assure us it would be renewed. The effect was to put my credit lines into arrears. This gave it the right to cross within the bank (pull all loan agreements personal and business) and call every single loan we had with it, including mortgages on homes and business real estate, vehicle loans, credit lines, everything. The failure to renew the line was the vehicle the bank used to effectively close me down! The credit line agreement included language to the effect that if I defaulted on the line, the bank could call every loan I had in five days. And this was exactly what it was doing. This was not a tactic used only by my bank. These were the same loan agreements used by banks across the country with small-business owners like me.

Evidently, it had been an elaborate setup from the beginning. It ensured that we would remain passive and confused as we were led to the chopping block. Now all it had to do was remove our heads.

However, I still didn't get it. I still didn't understand that the bank, my bank, had structured the very situation it needed to call my loans, all while assuring me everything would be fine. Thinking this was so ludicrous it had to be a mistake, I contacted my attorney. He set up a meeting for us the next day with a bankruptcy attorney.

Sheryl and I collected the paperwork we needed and met with the bankruptcy attorney the next day. We related the entire story, and he said the best thing we could do at that point was for him to prepare a letter to send to the bank informing it that if it continued on this course, he would take me through bankruptcy. The bank replied that he should go ahead. It did not plan to stop its proceedings. Only later did I find out that it was under direct orders from the FDIC to get our loans off its books, no matter the cost. That meant, of course, no matter the cost to *us*, no matter the cost to our long-term banking relationship, no matter the destruction wreaked upon our businesses and our lives.

How quickly, it seemed, the very agencies that should have been looking after our interests became our adversaries. It was not unlike when the Titanic was sinking and some men were putting themselves in the lifeboats before women and children. Those who we thought were our protectors were now desperately focused on only saving themselves while leaving us and thousands of others to drown.

Our world was in free fall. Sleep was difficult if not impossible. We were still looking after several elderly parents in declining health. We were faced with losing our home and our businesses. My mother, my reliable safety net for so long, had been gone for ten years. The strain was becoming imposing. We had no idea what we were going to do. It was the most isolating feeling in the world. The world was collapsing around us like something from a disaster movie. We stood to lose in a flash everything we had worked for our entire lives. It was incomprehensible.

The bank was closing in. We had already received its letters of repossession and foreclosure. The first thing it did was repossess our vehicles. The bank took our service trucks! This effectively shut down our service business. I guess it didn't comprehend the fact that you can't run a service business without trucks. And if you can't run your business, you have no possible way to repay loans. More likely, in its own panic, it just didn't care. Remember, its orders from the FDIC were to get the paper (what bankers call the loan agreements) off its books.

My son, who worked for me at the time, was on a service call at a house about twenty miles from our office, and the bank had a recovery company take possession of the truck while he was in the house! He literally walked out of the house in time to see his truck being hauled away on a wrecker. It was hard to figure who was the more desperate, the banks or us. But it was clear who had the power. It wasn't us.

Our situation worsened day by day, but we did find one place for some relief. I legally sold to Sheryl our manufacturing company, Islands By Design. We had found a way she could salvage that particular business, but I would have to totally leave it and not be involved in any way. This was no scheme; Sheryl paid fair market value for the business. There was no other way to do it. The money she paid had to be paid to creditors. The business also had a loan of $100,000 from her, so she was included as a creditor in the upcoming bankruptcy filing like any other creditor.

Likely the wisest move Sheryl and I ever made was signing a prenuptial agreement prior to our marriage. Why did we do this, one was to protect her from liability if my company was ever sued, but the other was we never wanted to become enemies if we decided we were not right for each other. As such we signed the agreement prior to our marriage. It meant that we were individuals under the eyes of the law in the state of North Carolina. This allowed us to salvage something that we otherwise could never have kept. Needless to say, I would strongly advise any married persons in business to protect themselves in this way, but it must be done prior to marriage, and it must be legal in the state you live in. One thing is obvious: You need to protect yourself in every way you can from financial calamity. Neither the banks nor anyone else will have your back when it happens. It will be the most lonesome day of your life!

12

My World In Transition

I told my son to start his own business or go find a job. It was over. On March 23 at 9:25 a.m., I called a meeting of all of my employees. I told them that I was shutting down the companies, all of them. I was being forced out of business for lack of funding by the bank, and I was headed for bankruptcy. They all looked at me in shock, over forty of them. I then told them they had new jobs working with the new owner of IBD, Sheryl. I explained that she had bought the business.

I felt we had done the best we could for our employees. They could all continue to be employed with the same benefits and the same rate of pay. Our consciences were clear since we were able to keep our employees employed at a time when our situation was desperate and jobs were very scarce. You can imagine our shock when 85 percent of our workforce decided to quit. Some did not want to work for a woman; others hoped to hold her over a barrel and get more money. This was a group of people I had cared for like members of my family, and after all we had been through, they walked out. It's simply amazing how quickly friends can disappear when you are sinking in the waters of chaos.

We had orders to fill and no one to make the product. We were at a very low point. Nothing seemed to be going well.

But Sheryl is a winner; she proved it then, and she proves it still every day. She put it all back together. Within a few days, the systems we had established (after studying *The E-Myth* and writing standard operating systems) made it so much easier to restart. We had the plant back up and running within days, and finding workers was easy. Unemployment was climbing, and finding qualified people was very easy. We filled orders, and we made our deliveries. We had to. Our backs were against the wall. We had failed all we could. There was no room for us to fail further. We would have been destitute. I had always been a systems guy, with the how-tos for any task spelled out. This practice enabled Sheryl to build production up very rapidly and continue to fill orders. There were some lapses, but I think she truly excelled in her ability to forge ahead and not simply throw up her hands.

Unfortunately, there was still more bad news to come.

Everything will be OK in the end. If it's not OK, it isn't the end.

—JOHN LENNON

13

What Do We Do Next When All Seems Lost

In the end, no matter what, one must remember this is America. In America, if you are willing to go the distance and pull out all the stops, no matter where you start from, you can succeed.

I was now in the process of filing personal bankruptcy. As mentioned before, due to our premarital agreement, Sheryl did not have to file. Only I had signed the loan papers since only I had owned the businesses, however, several things happened:

1) We were presented a demand letter from one of the banks with which I had a $100,000 loan. This letter said that Sheryl had co-signed one of my notes and was, therefore, obligated to pay the loan, even if I defaulted. The bank provided a loan agreement showing her signature! But it was a forgery. We actually engaged the services of a handwriting expert to determine this. Someone at the bank had forged her signature!

2) In the summer of 2010, Sheryl was rebuilding IBD Outdoor Rooms using self-funding.

3) I was wondering what to do with my life. I could no longer be involved with Sheryl's operation for legal reasons. I had to chart a new course for myself. I sent out my résumé, looking for jobs in an industry I had worked in for a number of years. No opportunities revealed themselves—none at all. It was hard to believe. I was a recognized expert in the industry, an industry leader, and at fifty-six years old I was not hirable. No one wanted me!

So instead, during that summer, as Sheryl was building IBD Outdoor Rooms for the future, I started to put together a plan to open a consulting company. Over the previous several years I had often been hired as an expert witness in legal cases. I thought I might pursue that as a full-time endeavor. The calls for my legal services as an expert witness had just come out of nowhere over the years. It paid well. Perhaps it was time to move into a completely new realm of work and a new profession.

During this time, our personal income was minimal, and it was getting harder and harder to make ends meet. However, the entire time I had been self-employed, I had paid unemployment tax on myself. That meant I was qualified to receive unemployment compensation. So for the first time in my life, I filed for unemployment and received the sum of $423 a week. It was all Sheryl could do to hold IBD together, so this money made it possible for us to survive this period. But here I am, one day I am the CEO of corporations, multiple employees and in only a few short month I am drawing unemployment compensation from the state of North Carolina.

By August of 2010, we had completed as much prep work as we could for the bankruptcy, and the attorney filed for it. We had been told by our legal counsel that this would be a pretty seamless process. It would be filed, we would need to attend some legal proceedings, and in ninety days it would all be over and life could begin anew. It was supposed to be a kind of financial rebirth. It sounded very good. Well, like everything else about this situation, that was only part of the story. How little did we realize what was going to happen and the lawsuits from banks we would be required to fight in court just to get our simple bankruptcy finalized. This advice, that the process would be simple and straightforward, failed to inform us of all the ways it could be contorted, frustrating, humiliating, aggravating, and difficult.

Over the next two months, I attended a hearing on my bankruptcy. Adding insult to injury, I also had to attend the required classes on how to restructure my financial life. I wonder if any of the Wall Street bankers who caused the crash of the world markets were required to take any classes. Talk about having to endure another humiliating experience in what was beginning to seem like an endless stream of blows to what little pride we had left.

One of the things you are required to do while going through bankruptcy, you have to attend a bankruptcy hearing. It is here that anyone comes forward who wants to contest the bankruptcy or feels the need to talk to the bankruptcy trustee. My hearing was in a room full of others who were also having their hearings. During those hearings, I heard numerous cases that made me feel I had entered a very bizarre world. The vast majority of those people had amassed a lot of credit card debt; that was it. They had no assets to take, no businesses to lose, no houses to forfeit. They had simply overextended themselves in a credit-easy world.

When my case was called, the trustee asked me a few questions, and my attorney answered them in the way they were supposed to be answered. Pretty cut and dried. We left thinking all was well. Even the attorney felt we should be able to close this in the following thirty days as no one had submitted anything to protest or object to my bankruptcy. Wrong again. One of the banks with which I held a $100,000 credit line decided to challenge my bankruptcy. I also found out that the flat fee I had paid entering the bankruptcy was not going to cover this challenge. My bankruptcy attorney was going to bill me $450 an hour to represent me against this threat!

Feeling hopeless and full of despair is a slower way of being dead.

—Author unknown

That bank filed for the opportunity to examine me in a deposition. This was set up in my attorney's office. For two hours I was questioned relentlessly about my business, my financial life, my son's business, and my wife's business. He also questioned me about every gift I had ever made to family members, especially those during the twenty-four months prior to the filing. It seems the court has the right to track back years prior to your filing for bankruptcy. If it sees gifts, if it sees that some have gotten paid and others have not, the court can take possession of those gifts. It was at this time that a motorcycle I had given Sheryl was challenged, and she had to either pay for the motorcycle or allow the bankruptcy court to take it. We scraped the money to buy it as we could buy it below value, but we only bought it to turn right around and sell it as we needed the cash. This was a period of time where we sold many personal items simply to stay afloat, things like food, electricity and other basic essentials.

During this time, we also discovered an interesting fact about the power of the bankruptcy laws. If someone with a higher amount than others, in other words, if someone had gotten paid and others did not, or some got a greater percentage what was owed while others did not, then the bankruptcy court had the right and the power to demand that this creditor pay the money back to the bankruptcy court as it was considered that the money paid the creditor had been paid with favoritism. Because of that, all of our credit card purchases and checks we had written were examined for this by the bankruptcy trustee, this to insure no one had gotten preferential paying. I well remember telling some that if we had the money and paid them, the court would have simply taken it back.

It was yet another low point, as we were now faced with losing Sheryl's possessions. And I also had unexpected bankruptcy-attorney bills mounting.

This same bank proceeded with its lawsuit. My bankruptcy could not be finalized until the suit was settled. So began a year of legal filings, meetings, and threats. The bank made all kinds of offers—such as my paying the amount owed to it over ten years or paying half immediately—and in return for agreeing to such an offer, it would drop the suit. The list was long. And to top all of that, I no longer had an attorney. He had filed with the bankruptcy court to drop me as a client. Perfect. I was abandoned by my attorney, the guy who had advised that this was going to be an easy, ninety-day process. He had said to me, "We file. In sixty days you will attend a hearing. You have to complete credit counseling. In ninety days life starts over. The cost for this is $3,750." That was more than an understatement. Maybe it worked that way in some other galaxy, but it was not even close to the way things went in this one.

Everything we hear is an opinion, not a fact.
Everything we see is a perspective, not the truth.

—MARCUS AURELIUS

14

You Are Now All Alone

During the hearing to allow my attorney to drop me, the judge said, "Mr. Isenhour, it is truly sad that in our system someone like yourself can find no help whatsoever. We cannot give you a court-appointed attorney. We cannot provide you any help. I am sad to say, sir, but you are on your own going forward." And with that, he approved my attorney's abandonment of me. Is there any more helpless feeling than to have your life at the mercy of the court system, and the person you have depended on to guide you through it simply walks away?

Walking out, I told the attorney I was really sorry I could not pay him. And he said something that blew me away. He said, "Jerry, you now have the best attorney money can buy! That judge has a soft side for people like you, people who busted their butts, and the system killed them and caused them to be here. You are the victim of the bad deeds of others. I could certainly have stayed on your case and hoped one day to be paid. But to be honest, you are better without me. If you have no attorney, the judge will know you are against the wall and that you are not trying to hide anything or steal from the system. You are simply a major victim. And this is the best thing for you."

As he walked off, I wondered, no attorney? How in the world is this the best thing?

> *Being alone with your feelings is the worst because you have nowhere to run. They are here in your head dancing, and all you can do is handle them as best you can.*
>
> —Author unknown

But not all the news was bad. By this time we had accumulated enough information about home foreclosures to discover how we might keep one of our homes. It had to do with the low amount of equity we had in the home. To prove this, we had to research through the courthouse the value of our house, the percentage of what it was worth on the market compared to the value it had been assigned for tax purposes, and other houses in the local market to see what the courthouse steps value was (what the property would bring in a foreclosure sale). Like everything else about this process, it wasn't easy. Foreclosures were resulting in the selling of homes at approximately 65 percent of the values estimated for property tax purposes.

To establish a value for the home we kept, we had to analyze foreclosures over the past twenty-four months and compare these to the average drop below the listed tax value. In the end, thankfully, we were able to keep one home. But motor-cycles, cars, and everything else went bye-bye.

I attended foreclosure hearings on my mortgages. I learned a lot about banks and credit lines and how the bank had been able to legally call every loan I had. It was eye-opening to see so clearly into the system. And it was pretty clear, in this particular case, that the system was not built to work in my favor.

If you want a sense of how far you have fallen, attend a courthouse steps auction where your property is being sold to the highest bidder. The bank's attorney conducts the auction. He reads a whole bunch of words out loud whether or not anyone is there and then enters the bank's bid, enough to cover its loan. If someone is willing to pay more, that person can buy it. If the bank is the higher bidder, it then owns it. If you remember the years of foreclosures from 2008 and onward, this was the process; people were buying foreclosed homes. Many investors with cash money got rich on this.

I often wondered whether they understood or even cared that they had just purchased someone's hard-earned dream. Even today, as I ride by any of my properties that were sold, it is hard to look at them. These were my dreams, these were my retirement, and these were the result of my hard work. The saddest and most baffling part was that the properties were sold for much less than we owed the banks. That was a hard and bitter pill to swallow.

I ride by my former fireplace shop and outdoor living retail center, sometimes I even pull in the parking lot and gaze. It seems so long ago, but how well I remember the blood, sweat, and tears we poured into that place. How well I remember when money was tight and I could not pay myself, how I ended up loaning that money back to the company. When it was all said and done I was owed several hundred thousand dollars by my own corporations, money I would never see. And money my wife borrowed and loaned to the corporations, money she likewise would never see.

How well I remember another person where the bank attorney was also selling his home and farm on the courthouse steps that day at the same time. This farm had been in his family for years, and the financial crisis forced him to lose his home, his farm, his entire world. I watched as his neighbors sat there watching. They did not come to buy; they did not come to support; they simply came to watch, to see who would be the new owner. It was similar to going to a fight of the gladiators during the Roman Empire, where men entered the field of combat and people came just to see the blood and the death.

When you have to cope with a lot of problems, you're either going to sink or you're going to swim.

—Tom Cruise

Without an attorney, I had to represent myself in the foreclosure hearings that were held (though Congressman Lawrence Kissell assigned an aide to attend the hearings with me). I had no experience as an attorney, but I had been through a lot of legal proceedings over the years and knew enough legal procedure to thoroughly frustrate the bank attorney. That, at least, provided a small amount of satisfaction. I also had several friends who were attorneys who assisted me with advice, these were the friends that were there when you were down, I mean really down. Being able to frustrate a bank attorney gave me a sincere amount of satisfaction, at least I was making him earn his fees!

How did a US congressman get involved? Before the hearings, I had requested and gotten an appointment with my local congressman. I explained the dilemma of how the bank had effectively shut us down and caused us to add people to the rolls of the social welfare system and how it seemed we were losing our home and our lives. He assigned a congressional aide to work with us. This aide attended the foreclosure hearings with me. The congressional office said it had never experienced anything like this, they did not even realize a bank could do what this bank was doing. It proved to be a learning experience for them, a much more painful lesson for us.

When you go through dire situations like this, you consider yourself the biggest loser who ever walked the face of the earth. You challenge your own purpose. It is a time for soul-searching, a time to look hard into the crevices of your life and evaluate what you find there. It is not easy, but you instinctively find you need to do so.

> *He who asks a question is a fool for a minute; he who does not is a fool for a lifetime.*
>
> —ANCIENT CHINESE PROVERB

More unpleasant news came at us. My son, who had started his own company by then, was also named in a lawsuit by the bank. It claimed he was fronting for me by continuing my chimney sweep business under a new name.

Sheryl was sued by the bank for the same reason. Both of them had to get attorneys to resolve these groundless claims.

Needless to say, all of this simply added to the stress that continued, unabated, day after day. It was ugly. It was hugely discouraging, and it was hard to imagine a way out.

During this time, the bank that sued Sheryl and my son was, unbelievably, also trying to get me to continue paying it the money I owed it even after the bankruptcy. This went on for months as letters and legal demands went back and forth like artillery barrages. Finally, after a period of time, the bank dropped its claims in return for me dropping mine. The details of this settlement are sealed, but let's just say dropping it was in the best interests of all. And dropping it meant we could *finally* move forward with our lives, which had been in limbo for way too long.

During all of this, I had arranged a face-to-face meeting with US Senator Richard Burr. He listened to my story and shared how the banking issue had affected his own family because of his wife's real estate business. He shared with me how the Senate felt helpless and unable to make any changes because of the strength of the anti-banking lobby and the Dodd-Frank bill. That particular bill had some unintended and very unpleasant consequences. Some of the language in the bill substantially contributed to the loss of loan opportunities for business owners. Portions of this bill quite simply halted any way for a person with an entrepreneurial spirit to build, as it effectively eliminated that person's path to any type of loans for building a business. But that's another story—about how legislation can poison the very water it is meant to clean.

At this point, life was beating me down hard! It is difficult to admit, but it wasn't easy to avoid thoughts of just ending the pain. More than once, these thoughts visited me. But I knew to do this would be crushing for Sheryl and my kids and would affect their lives forever. This, and my own determination to survive, helped me resist those impulses during that dark time. Even so, I wondered if my life would ever resume as before. The pain and the humiliation were so hard to bear, even to appear in public was really uncomfortable. I felt like a failure, and I had always been a winner (or so I thought). These are the times one cannot even think clearly, and even compassion for others seems to dry up. You feel utterly defeated, utterly crushed.

Crossing paths with people who asked about what happened only added to the feeling of hopelessness. Their questions were numerous: "I see you closed your shop. Are you enjoying retirement?" And each and every time I faced this question, I asked myself whether I was really a failure, as all seemed to see. Was I really a person who just had no idea what I was doing and got myself into this fine mess? *If* I just wasn't around, would the world be better? I can only say that the saving grace for me was the support I kept getting from Sheryl. It is not in the good times that you realize how much someone cares. It is in the depths of the worst times when you know someone cares.

It was late during this summer of 2010 that I filed for unemployment insurance. Nothing makes you feel quite as much like a failure as having to collect unemployment after you've owned your own businesses and been held in high esteem by the industry you worked in. But it was a matter of survival then, so I collected the unemployment check weekly until December. (I guess I didn't have to feel too badly about it since it was, in essence, my own unemployment insurance that I had paid that was being paid back to me. But it was still humiliating.)

But it was also shocking to see how easy this was and how evident the failure of the system was. To collect the unemployment money, there were no requirements of me, except to file weekly, and the unemployment office made that easy because you could do it every Sunday evening, and on Tuesday you would have another $423 in your account to spend as you saw fit. There were no questions about where I was applying and no requirement to apply for jobs. I was simply dumbfounded, simply keep filling out the form every Sunday night, and you get a check, the only requirement was to file that form every Sunday evening. Was it any wonder that this system of unemployment insurance, through which people received weekly money for just being alive, was ruining our country? I see this all too often, and I experienced it firsthand; it is way too easy to simply live off the system.

I discovered that my unemployment benefits would stop if I were to become self-employed again. I could keep drawing unemployment, or I could reestablish myself. The whole idea of this unemployment insurance seemed turned on its head. Instead of helping someone get back on his or her feet, it seemed designed to keep the person in the hole. The system made it real easy; you got a debit card, and the money was there every Tuesday to spend as you pleased. However, I decided to open a bank account (with very meager funds) and start again, even though it meant having to forego the unemployment benefits we really needed. It was then I formed my new business, Chimney & Venting Consultants. I was relaunched in November of 2010 and on my way to a new career.

My total income in 2010 was about $5,000. Hardly anything to brag about or even be sustained by. It was a big change for a guy who used to have large lines of credit and who could simply call the car dealership and get whatever he wanted, but it was a beginning. And that is what I needed.

15

A New Life Begins

I embarked on my new career as a consultant on fireplaces and chimneys for the hearth, chimney, and legal industries. Though it was producing very limited income at the time, at least I had an occupation, a purpose and something to hope for. And on the emotional level, that was an important compensation. It made me feel I had a purpose again, some direction, something to keep my self-esteem from total annihilation. I had work.

It was a long winter with no income. I lived off my wife's earnings. My presence in her business would have been an issue for her, so I had to steer clear. I had a few close friends I could talk to—my buddy Ken Warren and my old friend Greg Polakow—but nothing could totally ease my feeling of isolation. This was a very lonesome period of time, and likely the one thing that held my sanity together was the love that Sheryl had for me.

The executive director of an association of which I had been president contacted me early in the year 2011. I had previously alerted him to the ordeal I was going through. He asked me if I planned to go to the association's annual meeting in Hartford, Connecticut, in February. I told him probably not, that I was not up to it, that I just didn't think I could do it. Sheryl also asked me a few days later if I was going. I gave her the same answer. She told me I really should go because the organization was planning a special event for two of my friends from the industry who had passed away. I told her I was really not up to it. Mark, the executive director, contacted me again. He said the association really wanted me to come. Finally, after repeated requests, I agreed to go for the banquet only.

The night of the banquet was hard. I felt as if all eyes were on me, judging me. I walked into the hotel that Saturday afternoon hoping no one would see me. I felt eyes on me from every direction. I felt people were cynically smiling at me because I had proven myself a gigantic failure. I believed they must consider me a person who had fallen and that I had failed due to my own stupidity, my own blunders in business, my poor judgment, etc. It was so uncomfortable. For the first time in my life, I felt ill at ease around my friends and around an industry to which I had devoted many years as a leader. I felt more like a failure at the outset of that evening than at any point in my life. My heart was heavy and tears of embarrassment and humiliation were hard to fight back. "Panic attack" would pretty accurately describe what I was experiencing.

During the banquet, the President of the NCSG announced the forthcoming presentation of an award that had only been given once before in the history of the Association. I felt this must be about some recognition for my departed friend Pete Luter. His wife Emily, and Paul one of his sons were there. Or possibly another recently departed dear friend, Jack Pixley, was going to get a posthumous award. Either of these would have made perfect sense, and I would have been happy if either of those two guys had been recognized. They both had done a huge amount for the industry.

However, to my immense surprise, my name was called as the winner of the Lifetime Achievement Award for the industry. I was absolutely floored. Nothing could have surprised me more than this. This award had only been presented on a single occasion in the past thirty years! Not only was I the second recipient, I was the only living recipient. To say I was speechless is an understatement. I wept. I was unable to utter a single word for quite a while. This gesture by the industry revealed more than anything else could have that the people of this industry, my industry, were genuinely grateful for all I had done. It was an immense honor. One I still cherish deeply, even as I write this page a tear comes to my eye as I remember that evening.

That evening remains in my memory as one that gave me new hope after such a long period of dismay and gloom. As I looked across the table, I realized the others sitting with me were aware I was going to be honored in this way. They were watching for my reaction. I'm not sure what they expected, but I know speaking was difficult at that moment. I could do nothing at first but remain in my chair, overwhelmed by so many feelings, trying to compose myself, trying to collect my thoughts and feelings.

Randy Brooks, the president of the association, whispered to me as I walked up to receive this award. He told me no one was going to let me go through life without knowing how deeply everyone appreciated my dedication to the industry. He wanted, above all else, for me to know the difference I had made in his life and in the lives of countless others who made their living, as I did, in the industry. Likely he never even realized at the time how powerful those words to a man who had been beaten to a pulp as I had!

His words were a tonic to my spirit and my self-esteem. I wanted him to know how they ignited my heart and my mind. How they carried the unmistakable, unforgettable message that someone cared. Because prior to that evening, it had seemed that the people who cared were few and far between, I felt I had been forgotten. Public speaking was never difficult for me, but that night, overwhelmed with emotions, the ability to speak had been sucked from my being like oxygen sucked from a roaring fire. My heart was filled with gratitude, but I could find no words there to express what I was feeling.

I don't know if anyone there realized it, but that award, perhaps as nothing else could have, propelled me forward to a new purpose in life, a new life mission, and a new destiny. Only shortly before, I had been pondering if it was time for me to remove myself from this world. And yet, that night, at a hotel banquet for a small trade organization, suddenly my life started to hold meaning and value and purpose once again. This is the kind of lifesaving power such gestures hold. It was a breath of new life for me. Even today, as I write this, tears fill my eyes as

I recall that large room of people and the clear realization that they cared; they really cared. And I sensed at that moment in time a renewed sense of what my purpose was in life, I just had not put all the pieces together at that point.

To be honest, the only thing up to this point that had kept me on the planet was the unconditional love, dedication, and support from my wife. She was my rock. Love is always easy when things are good, but true love, the love one feels through thick and thin, only comes when the person you love cares for you no matter what you do or say, no matter what is going on in your life, no matter what circumstances fate has presented. And Sheryl showed that kind of love for me throughout every minute of that time.

Her support was the single thing that kept me going and allowed me to stand in front of people without the shame I had been feeling for so long. While I felt shame about what had happened, at that point I was totally oblivious that this evident failure was going to be a game changer. And as I see so clearly now, it was one of the most magnificent and consequential moments of my life.

16

Personal Reinvention Begins

The greatest difficulty always comes right before the birth of a dream.

—Joel Osteen

This was the moment when reinvention began for me. This was when the dismantling of my life was going to end. This was my time to turn the tables and move forward again. I realized, finally, no one but I could make it happen.

But this was also the time it occurred to me, this entire scenario was not the bank's fault, it was no one else's fault, this was my fault, my fault for the ways that I did not see, could not see that my enemy was within. An enemy that would not allow me to see myself.

It is fascinating to note that reinvention would not have been possible without the chaos that had to come first. It came to tear down the old structure of my life so something new could be built in its place. The chaos led to a hugely important lesson: We ourselves create our failures and successes. We can overcome the most dire circumstances and reversals if we have character, determination, grit, and vision. I learned that often the whole value of this kind of chaos is to lead us forward to a new purpose and a new meaning for our lives, new avenues of progress, new successes. Sometimes you just have to be patient and know that even when times are darkest, things will get better. The only thing to do until that happens is to continue to move forward even when it seems impossible. The one thing you can never do is quit.

> *You may not realize it when it happens, but a kick in the teeth may be the best thing in the world for you.*
>
> —WALT DISNEY

Even today, in my capacity as a coach, I realize the process of moving toward one's dreams must often be preceded by the understanding that we are frequently our own worst enemy. The failure to see ourselves clearly in the mirror, accept our flaws, and then change may well be our number one obstacle to success in life and in business.

It has also been an eye-opening experience to realize that the person who is very lucky in life, is the person who can look in the mirror and see where they need to change. And, how we are so often held back, not allowed to reach our dreams until we face, endure, and deal with significant pain. This can be seen in all phases of life.

I have often heard that an Alcoholic can never beat that disease (and it is a disease,) until they hit bottom, until all is lost. That's why I have found I truly admire those individuals who can grasp that they are the cause of all of their own problems.

One of my clients, a guy named Mark Stoner, a gifted charismatic individual, and mentor to many (including myself even though he is my client), shared with me the following gold nugget. When a person has a crappy business, it is not the fault of the market, his people or his product. Mark shared that the reason that someone has a crappy business is because they themselves are a crappy business owner. They allowed the business to be crappy! Mark was a very wise man, he thought this out and set to work on his own business model, making statements saying it is all my fault are tough to do, and then tell an audience, and even write about it as he has in his book Blue Collar Gold, is a phenomenal way of sharing with others the hard lessons you have learned that can help another human being!

The same can be said when someone has a crappy life. Usually, it's because they allow their life to be crappy, and they never do anything about it!

> *If today were the last day of my life, would I want to do what I am about to do today?*
>
> —STEVE JOBS

The next morning Sheryl and I had breakfast with a man with whom, at that moment, I was undoubtedly meant to be with. I think God guided this friend to meet with me at that important time. He is a man I had been friends with for years. That morning, because of his words of encouragement, his abiding friendship, support, and love, I was bolstered even more. That man was John Meredith, and like most of my friends by that time, he knew of the issues I'd been dealing with. He learned even more of the details that day.

During breakfast, I revealed to John my plans for the consulting endeavor. Hearing this, he said, "Jerry, these guys (in this industry) need you. You need to become a coach." He told me that my unique insight, experience, and leadership were what others needed to help them face their own challenges. He believed I could help a lot of people as a coach and mentor. His words were inspiring mostly because they were so sincere. John, along with Sheryl, truly believed in me, and they both let me feel that belief at a time I needed it most.

I know that for quite a few years, in fact until I asked John to review this book for me, that he even realized the effect he had on me, how his words had been the words of strength I needed so badly to hear. Today I travel through Hartford quite often, and each time I do I think back to the day in 2011, that day of a reinvention and a refocusing of my purpose in life.

Driving back to Boston that day to board a plane to Charlotte, I felt a fire in my belly and in my mind. I had a purpose once again. I had a mission. And I had something else—the knowledge and supreme confidence I was going to make this work.

As buoyed as I was by the events at the banquet and my breakfast with John, we still had very little income except what Sheryl was producing. The bank had taken many of our possessions, and we had sold as much as we could of what remained. You know your finances are meager when you wear a pair of tennis shoes even when they've worn out. Goodwill had become our favorite store.

In this pretty severe financial crunch, I began to build my new career as a business coach. I would ultimately brand myself as a blue-collar business coach with a specialization in the home service provider trades. Using websites and social marketing and working with meager resources, we began to build the process of new dreams and new directions for my life.

But the reality of the day was that I had a new dream, a new purpose, a new direction. But even with these, there was no business, no client base, and nothing to expand upon. But did I care? No, I didn't, the reason was, for the first time in a long time, I now had a direction, a purpose, and the knowledge that someone believed in me once again. And that was enough to fuel the fire that was now burning inside of me.

17

They Will Come For Your Home

Meanwhile, the payments on our home were strangling Sheryl. We could not sustain them. We had earlier tried to sell that house, to no avail. I still had no income. We were in a jam.

So once again we contacted our local congressional office and learned of a program for people like us. A congressional aide told us we qualified for a HAMP loan modification program. He instructed us to file with our bank for that. So off to the bank we went, to file the numerous pages of information to get a loan modification that would allow us to keep our house. Then there was nothing to do but wait for the call from the bank. Several anxious weeks later, we were contacted by a representative of the bank.

Unbelievably, inconceivably, and without any logic, we were told by the bank official that we did not make enough money to qualify for a loan payment reduction! Let me say that again. We didn't make enough money to qualify for a loan payment reduction. It was like the bank missed the whole point. I mean, if we had had more income, we would not have needed the reduction! Could anything anywhere have been more ridiculous? Here we were making the outrageous payments that were three times larger than the modification would have been, and we were told we did not qualify to make lower payments because we did not have enough income! I didn't even know what to say.

There was no way in hell I was going to settle for that answer. With a little probing, I discovered the problem was not that I did not make enough money to qualify but rather that there was nothing in it for the bank. (Wow. They just never fail to disappoint!) They simply were not going to make it happen. That was a pretty easy process for them and yet another example of them climbing into the lifeboat ahead of everyone else.

However, by some miracle, one of the bank officers had worked with my mother years previously when she worked at a bank. When he learned of my plight, he pulled the needed strings at the bank, and our house payment was reduced by over 60 percent, in effect saving our home which likely would have also gone to foreclosure at some point.

Later we learned that very few people ever succeeded in getting that loan reduction. I guess banks just found it easier to repossess a house and resell it than to work with their current customers so they could keep their houses.

We can't help everyone, but everyone can help someone.

—RONALD REAGON

The process lowered our interest rate to a very low level for a period of five years. Finally a positive financial step. Was this an intervention by my mother? Undoubtedly. Without her, intentionally or otherwise, I would never have had a connection to this man, and we would have lost our house. I'm sure this was one more instance of my mother acting as my safety net, even long after she had left this earth.

18

The Banks Are Controlled
By An Unseen Force

This same man, a chief financial officer for a major bank, explained to me the process of how the bank's control comes from sources over which we have no control. The FDIC controls the banks by the cost of the FDIC insurance. If the banks don't follow the FDIC guidelines, the FDIC raises rates on insurance and can even withhold insurance coverage. Without that insurance, a bank cannot operate. Period.

Next, he explained to me how the FDIC was controlled by the Federal Reserve System, which is controlled by no one but itself. The Federal Reserve can at any time choose to raise the interest rate at which the bank borrows money. Obviously, it was well outside the normal system of checks and balances we assume is overriding all of what our government does. The Board reports to and is directly accountable to the Congress but, unlike many other public agencies, it is not funded by congressional appropriations. In addition, though the Congress sets the goals for monetary policy, decisions of the Board—and the Fed's monetary policy-setting body, the Federal Open Market Committee—about how to reach those goals do not require approval by the President or anyone else in the executive or legislative branches of government. That is what it was d to be designed to be when it was envisioned by a group of the nation's wealthiest people, created by Congress with the Federal Reserve Act, and signed by President Woodrow Wilson in 1913.

These facts were confirmed during my meetings with US congressmen, US senators, and the North Carolina State Banking Commission. I found we were pawns of the banking system once we let them get their hooks in us. This is the very information I needed to assist my clients in ensuring they would never be in the position I was in.

I have been asked on several occasions what qualifies me to assist others in business since I failed. Some of these have been questions, others to be honest in a way that my counsel should never be seriously considered, after all, I had failed. My answer is that it is the very fact that I failed that allows me to know firsthand how that happens. I understand failure because I did fail and in such a massive way. Armed with that knowledge permanently imprinted in my brain, I will never sit idly by and watch a client go through what I went through. I will use every resource at my command, all of my experience, and all of my skill to protect my clients from the same trap I fell into.

Learn to control yourself, lest you be controlled by others.

—Author unknown

In other words, my failure is actually a strength my clients can lean on and learn from. This is why I encourage my clients to build bankable businesses. I want them to structure their businesses so that when push comes to shove, they can tell the bank that they don't need it. That is the only way the Fed cannot control your destiny!

You see, one of the things I learned in all of this was that for a business to have the highest value and to be the strongest, the business can borrow money from a bank without a personal guarantee from the owner/owners! Once you reach this level, you own a business of the highest value, one that is considered bankable.

One of the additional things that indicate you may have trouble ahead and a business that is too dependent on you is when you borrow money and they bank requires you to carry a life insurance policy with them as the beneficiary. This, in simple terms, means that you as the owner are the only thing that the bank is depending on. And the bank requires this insurance as the bank does not plan to lose in case you get hit by a bus!

19

The World Starts To Show Clarity

One day a few weeks after I had received the award that started my reinvention, I got a phone call from my friend John Meredith. He wanted to hold a seminar for his dealers. We scheduled a three-day training in Richmond, Indiana, for that spring. But he had an even bigger surprise; he wanted *me* to do the majority of the presentation. It was to be called "How To Obtain the Lion's Share of Business In Your Market." Furthermore, he wanted to pay me the entire proceeds from the seminar! That is the kind of person John is, generous and thoughtful beyond words. I was elated and excited by this offer. I had received hardly any income in the more than six months since I had opted to become self-employed rather than continuing to get unemployment compensation. (What a great way to rebuild America. As long as you want to sit on your butt, we'll send you a check every month. But if you start a business, you are on your own. What is the message here?)

So John promoted the seminar. It was entitled Changing Your DNA: Grabbing The Lions Share Of Business In Your

Market. John set this up with me as the main speaker and others in the industry doing smaller parts. How well I remember starting that seminar from the front of that room, pouring it on during my time on stage, and feeling that I was where I had always been intended to be, teaching others and helping them see how to move to their dreams.

I knew, standing in front of that room filled with my colleagues, that I had a message that others wanted and needed to hear. It was a message they could take home with them and use to make improvements to their business models and themselves that would assist them in reaching their dreams in life. This belief in myself fueled me to deliver a message in a way that could change lives!

We had a good turnout, and when it was over John handed me the largest check I had seen in a really long time. It was enough to substantially support my move toward being a business coach. John had told me at that breakfast back in Hartford that the guys and gals of this industry needed me. And now we finally had something concrete to show that I could, indeed, add value. And he had helped to make all that happen. John proved to me that I could truly help others reach their dreams!

As I look back at that period of time, I was able to see where I had delivered a seminar to a roomful of people, a seminar that could change their business DNA and move them towards their dreams of success. In fact, over the coming years, several of the people in that room that week actually signed up as my clients and are still clients to this day for my coaching and teaching services. And it was from this beginning that the formative thoughts in my mind were formed for a new career, a career that unknowingly I had been preparing for my entire life. It would be a career where my failures would be the strength that would help others reach their dreams and prevent them ever falling into the abyss of failure where I myself had fallen.

Often I wonder, do my clients know what I learn from each of them. Do they realize the knowledge they share with me and how much their support of me drives me to the next day and to what I consider my own dreams?

Driving home from Richmond, I was on top of the world. The seminar had gone well. I had received payment. I had actually been paid to speak and present to others. The whole process gave me a view of the future, my future, a clear path forward. I also had some funding to start building. You can do a lot with hope, desire, and good wishes, but somewhere along the way to build a business you need some actual cash to operate. Thanks to John Meredith, I now had some. The following quote I feel describes John more adequately than any person I have ever known:

> *You can have everything you want in life if you will simply help enough people get what they want.*

> —Zig Ziglar

Furthermore, my very first coaching client was another outcome of this seminar. Soon another materialized—and another. Over the next year, bit by bit, I began to build a base of coaching clients. I found that my ideas, processes, experience, and insights—all I had learned in building strong businesses over the years and all I had learned in seeing them destroyed—were, indeed, valuable to others. I was on my way.

But even more importantly, as I started working with one client, the things I learned helped me to help another. And today, CVC Coaching is a business built solidly through the testimonials that our clients give us. I think one of the most heartfelt testimonials was when a client told others, "I think Jerry cares more about my success than I do." To be honest, that is my mission. I want every single one of them to live the dreams they have. They share their wins and losses with me, and it goes beyond a client relationship; many times these clients become a part of my extended family.

As I build my services as a coach to others, one of the things that is like a dose of rocket fuel to me, are the words my customers share with me and with others. They see my value, and they credit their growing success to the contributions I made to them. This is such a tremendous feeling of excitement and pride, to see people reaching their dreams, and it continually drives me to exceed their expectations.

Today when I see one of my clients who has reached his or her dreams and goals, it is like looking at a trophy, a trophy of a hard-won victory. And each and every time I see one falter, I reach down, down deep into my mind and my being, and try to provide that person with the tools needed to assure that it's possible to drive forward once again.

Eventually, I was even able to start to rebuild my broken credit, though it was a lengthy and difficult process. The first credit card I applied for after our big crash came with a $125 application fee, a high annual fee, and a credit line of a measly $350! It wasn't great, but it was a start. This may not seem like a huge deal, but after having had all my credit cards taken and then only having one that Sheryl guaranteed, it meant a lot to me.

> *So take a deep breath, pick yourself up, dust yourself off, start all over again.*
>
> —DOROTHY FIELDS

20

Coaching, Helping Others Reach Their Dreams Becomes My Mission In Life

As I grew in my new business, I realized I needed more credentials. I began to seek out ways to move to the next level of authority. This training was not inexpensive, but I considered it an investment in the business. After all, if I was not committed to my own improvement, how could I expect my clients to be committed to theirs? If I was to be taken seriously as a coach, mentor, and advisor, then I had to show some evidence beyond my copious experience that I was committed, qualified, and trained for this.

But it was tough; many of the programs I was entering cost more than my total income for 2010 had been. And once you've been lowered to nothing, you look really hard at expenditures going forward. Those of us who were crippled by the events of 2008 now understand why our grandparents, who had lived through the Great Depression of the 1930s, evolved into what they became.

I reviewed a lot of the coaching programs and decided on the training and certification program offered by Jeffrey Gitomer. This involved some prep and some class time and, of course, writing some checks to pay for the training, but this provided me with the credentials and authority to show that I was investing in my own training to assist others with their own needs for moving forward and to their dreams. But I pursued this with the idea of perfecting the art of sales and how to connect with others. This was a skill I needed to build and could share with others who also needed this. Was there a big gulp to write these checks, you better believe it! But I viewed it as an investment... an investment in myself and added tools to assist my clients. You see you don't really know what you don't know until someone shows you the things they have learned. By working with experts one on one like this, I was able to share their wisdom shared with me with others.

But this was about far more than appearances. In fact, the whole process of gaining these certifications forced me to take an even harder look at who I was, the mistakes I had made, and gave me the goal of changing in ways that I had never envisioned. Looking back at my earlier years I now see why I failed to reach one of my earlier dreams, to retire at 50. But, to be honest, as I am now in my 60s, I have found that as one discovers what they truly love to do, retirement no longer remains the goal. You want to keep going, sharing with and helping others reach their dreams in life. It is the source of a really good feeling to watch those you are allowed the privilege to mentor reach their own dreams in life! It is like trophies, and to see this provides me an enormous sense of pride

There is a mixture of business owners I work with now, some are new, some are nearing the exit point in their business lives, others simply have never moved their businesses to the level they envisioned when they started. To be able to work with these people is such a satisfaction and provides such a high watching them move forward. It is pure satisfaction.

As I progressed as a coach working with small businesses in the blue-collar home services industry, it became very evident that many business owners faced a real challenge. They had other family members who were involved in the business and this caused a lot of stress to the business and to the family relationship. Because of that, we saw a need for training in that area. Sheryl was a natural for this, so she took her first step into the world of coaching (she had already been a coach in many ways to me and others), and she pursued her training through the Ziglar training and coaching system.

She moved to the position of a Ziglar Legacy Certified Trainer but did not stop there. Her next step was to proceed further with her study and training, and today it is with immense pride that I can introduce her as a Ziglar Certified Coach. And she has a close relationship to the Ziglar family, providing her the ability to consult with leaders such as Tom Ziglar and his sister Julie Ziglar Norman. After meeting these people at a Ziglar conference, I am certain that Sheryl has both the right stuff and the right training to help others with their challenges and the ability to help them achieve their dreams.

We envision doing joint presentations to groups on dreams, goals, and how people can live the lives they want. And to do this in a way that strengthens rather than strains our clients' personal relationships. I am really looking forward to the day when we can do joint presentations of this type.

I continued to take classes online and some in-person offerings, leading up to the next level I decided I wanted to pursue—being trained and certified as a leadership coach, speaker, and teacher under the number one leadership expert in the country, Dr. John Maxwell. I have gone through this training and was awarded this certification as a way of improving my offerings and my value to others.

Being able to promote myself as a John Maxwell certified trainer, coach, and speaker is something that I sit proud of today since it took a lot to get there. The number one part of the work, though, was the realization that the more I could learn and absorb, the more I would be able to help others reach their own personal and business dreams.

Ever since the day I began my career as a coach, I have communicated through social media, posting items of value for others. I do this based on the Ziglar philosophy and the ability to help others, no matter whether I have a personal gain from it. I live each day hoping to add value to the life of another human being and hoping to help someone live his or her own life dreams.

But not only does this training provide me the ability to assist others, it also gives valuable content that can be shared with others. A coach does not dream up new methods and concepts. Rather he shares what he learns from others. Being able to draw upon what I have learned from these coaching and training masters helps build value in the eyes of others of what I offer.

The future depends upon what we do in the present.

—MAHATMA GANDHI

But what one has to do, no matter who you are is realize that each and every day you must make moves to get better. And even though you can view your personal accomplishments with pride, understand, as humans, there are always ways to improve. And each of us also has to take advantages of these opportunities to improve.

This was the recent case with Sheryl and myself, we took advantage of an opportunity to study under another guy who has been a person who has inspired many of my thoughts. We recently completed a 3-day training program under Larry Winget, the Pitbull of Personal Development and as a team will be moving forward in the future under his tutelage also.

It was at this training that I saw a light go off in Sheryl, a new glow, she saw a new role for herself, one she can fill well, and she is preparing to add this to her own area of expertise as she is very experienced in this difficult task. Her new added mission of working with adults who are facing the difficult task of looking after parents as they start to depend more and more on their children due to the aging process. It is a difficult decision, and lifestyle choice, to look after parents as they age, but she carries the unique experience of having been there and done it, and how it wrecks emotional hell on the child and their spouse. Please understand, one of the things learned as we went this period of life is that life comes at us in cycles, there is our childhood, this the period our parents form our thoughts and look after us, providing the needs of life. We then enter adulthood, and now we are our own boss, setting our own destiny. But as we age, through the sheer aging process, we start to lose some of our abilities, and we now will commonly depend on our children to look after us, if we are lucky enough to have them, and they care! I know she will be truly phenomenal in this role, and my intent is to support her in this fully, after all, without her support and love would I even be able to write this book? I support her with pride, but how could I not, she is a phenomenal human being!

It remains such a pleasure to watch clients reaching their dreams, the ones who, such a short time ago, wondering how they were going to make payroll, that now are building their strategies of success, they are building reserves and building the businesses that they dreamed of. But this is done, not by myself or my team, rather it is done by a committed business owner who has decided they have had enough pain and it is time to see a gain!

21

Understanding The Journey

As I look back over the past few years of my life, I realize things that had never occurred to me during the years leading up to the day when financial chaos caused my life to crash. These are so clear to me today. It took me some years to realize this crash was an amazing and powerful event that transformed my life in ways that were both good and necessary.

As you view your youth and years as a young adult, as you move into the position of being viewed as a senior citizen, you look back at the life lessons learned, and you wonder why you were so often blinded.

Furthermore, though I had been in leadership for many years, I discovered I had made a lot of people angry with me. Many times I had said the wrong things in the wrong way. I had, in fact, caused many people to dislike and resent me. I had created adversaries in the process. This was due entirely to my actions, attitudes, and at times, utter disregard for people's feelings. It was quite a process for me to finally see this and admit to it. I am still working to rebuild that damage. Mistakes take a long time to correct. This realization did not come comfortably or easily, but it was one of the things that had to happen while reinventing myself and moving forward.

Oh yes, the past can hurt! But you can either learn from it or run from it.

—Rafiki, a character in *The Lion King* movie

In this reinvention, I also had to admit that I did not spend the time I should have with my children. I have come to accept that I may never be able to recoup those years and make up for that lost time. This is an especially harsh lesson to learn, but it is the sad result of, for whatever reason, always putting myself first, which can certainly be a major failing in one's life. There is nothing to do now but correct that flaw in my character and move on.

There is no job more important than parenting.

—Ben Carson

It is also quite apparent that many people are only interested in a friendship as long as it can help them. It is only when the chips are down that your true friends shine through.

Friendship is not about who you've known the longest. It's about who walked into your life, said "I'm here for you" and proved it.

—Author unknown

I have learned to listen more intently and openly to others. Only by doing that can we really understand not only who people are, but more importantly, the lessons we can learn from them. I know now that leaders listen, and when they speak, they speak with value so others will understand and want to hear more. They inspire. They uplift. And ultimately, they must genuinely care for the people they are leading.

A leader is one who knows the way, goes the way, and shows the way.

—John C. Maxwell

Armed with these new realizations and understandings, each morning I get up with the comfort of knowing that it is a new time for me, another chance to get it right. Happily, there is money in the bank. It's not borrowed money, as in the past, but the money I earned, deposited, and owe to no banks. Now, once again, we can afford to buy the things we need as well as the luxuries that make life comfortable. And that feels good, really good. This is such a comfort, and today I am able to work every day of my life, not because I have to (even though work is still a necessity), but because it is so much fun to work in a way that I truly love. At the same time, I have to place myself outside of my comfort zone daily, because when you stay in your comfort zone, your true potential will never be realized and lived.

Life begins at the end of your comfort zone.

—NEALE DONALD WALSCH

But there is something even more important than having secure finances once again and the ease they can bring. In the end, those are just side benefits to life. What is most important is to own up to and learn from your mistakes, to become a better person, to learn to stay grounded whatever is happening; to hold onto your vision; to trust and value your greatest wealth, which is a supportive family and your true friends; to persevere; and to never say die. Life is about growing, moving forward, changing, evolving. We should never allow any setback, no matter how chaotic, to interrupt that process.

My parting thoughts to you as you finish this book are some of the many things I have learned from others.

Zig Ziglar says, "If you help enough people get what they want, they will help you get what you want." I believe this is true. If you believe it and live it, great things will come to you. You will be a person who makes a difference in the lives of many others.

John Maxwell advises, "If you fail, fail forward. And if you are failing, realize that if you are to reach the top of the mountain you have to keep climbing no matter what the obstacles. When the climb gets hard, remind yourself to get back out there and engage. People need you." Often as humans, we fail so much more than we win, but to be the winner you can truly be, simply pick yourself up and dust yourself off, wipe away the dust, and move on again. You can do miraculous things, but only if you believe and continue onward.

Here's my philosophy in a nutshell: if you have something to give others, then make sure you do it. There are only so many days you are allowed to walk God's green earth. It is important to make each one count because, as corny as it may sound, life gets better when you help others.

It's true you can inspire people through your own failures, but you have to be willing to admit to your failures. You have to be able to stand up and say, "I screwed up. It was my fault." Yes, you may have failed, but that won't stop you from achieving your dreams. Remember to constantly look in the mirror and always strive to see yourself honestly—without the halos we like to put around our heads, without the excuses we make for being less than we can be—and always continue to improve. Whatever level of achievement we attain and however we conduct ourselves in the world, we can always get better. Doing so is what makes life rich.

Winners impart a gift to others when they speak of their own failures. So often we only hear of the success, and while we may think that success drives us, in reality, it is the failure of another and the knowledge of what they went through that will drive us to the hopes and dreams we each possess.

No matter what happens, no matter what failures you face, don't waste your time and energy blaming others. Look inside yourself and be determined to pick yourself up and get back in the game. It's good advice. It's truth. And it's the only way to live your life and fulfill your dreams. Dying can be a mental or a physical phenomenon—the process begins whenever you allow yourself to give up on life.

Life is too important not to live all of your dreams! Reinvention is continuous. Otherwise, you stagnate. You don't need to wait, as I did, for chaos to be your driving force.

With that I thank you. I thank you for taking time out of your life to read my story. If this book can change your life, if this book helps you reach your dreams, then my mission is complete. That was my mission in writing this, to change the lives of others, and I hope that yours will be one!

I close this with the words of one of the people I have studied under, and that is John Maxwell "Change yourself, before expecting change in others"

Made in the USA
Charleston, SC
03 March 2017